THE INVENTION OF CASTE HIERARCHY

THEORY IN HISTORICAL PERSPECTIVE

The Invention of Caste Hierarchy

Theory in Historical Perspective

GOMES da SILVA, J. C.

MOTILAL BANARSIDASS
INTERNATIONAL
DELHI

Delhi, ***2024***

ISBN : 978-81-972-9232-3

Also available at :
MOTILAL BANARSIDASS INTERNATIONAL
41 U.A. Bungalow Road, (Back Lane) Jawahar Nagar, Delhi-110007
4261/3 (Basement), Ansari Road, Darya Ganj, New Delhi-110002
203, Royapettah High Road, Mylapore, Chennai-600004
12/1A, 2nd Floor, Bankim Chatterjee Street, Kolkata - 700073

Stockist : Motilal Books Ashok Rajpath, Near Kali Mandir, Patna-800004

Printed in India by
MOTILAL BANARSIDASS INTERNATIONAL

To Teresa, a light on my path,
and to my daughters, Barbara and Sara

Contents

CHAPTER-1

INTRODUCTION
HISTORICAL CONTEXT

Any sociological work in India, unless it is very specialized, must necessarily take hierarchy into account.

- Louis Dumont

[Hierarchy is one of the images] through which anthropologists have frozen the contribution of specific cultures to our understanding of the human condition.

- Arjun Appadurai

I

When and how did "hierarchy" become a key word in the lexicon of Indianists?

Chaos, not hierarchy, is what 18th century European observers claimed to have found in India. Some acknowledged the *varna* hierarchy of ancient tradition (Brahmins, Kshatriyas, Vaishyas, Shudras), noting however that the *old state of social perfection no longer existed.* Moving away from the old model, India seemed to have renounced order altogether. For most Europeans of the time, order was founded on the absolute respect for rank and status: "To reverse the superiority of ranks, to reduce men to an imaginary equality (...) is a blaspheme against Providence", one author proclaimed (Ramsay 1722: 37-8, our translation).

Although this perspective had already been challenged, one of the main pillars of European rhetoric continued to be the deep-rooted opposition between Western "order" and Indian "chaos". Both terms were ideological constructions but the content imposed on the latter deserves particular attention.

Indian "chaos" was often conceived as a civilizational regression caused by the Biblical Flood, itself assimilated by certain 17th and 18th century authors to the conjectural transition from the state of nature to civil society. The gloomy colours of this picture were further accentuated, in the last third of the 18th century, by the ways in which some events in the history of the subcontinent were described and interpreted.

The disintegration of the Moghul Empire and the granting of the *Diwani* of Bengal, Bihar and Orissa to the East India Company in 1765 led to a dramatic power vacuum. The British were given the right to collect land revenue and exercise civil justice in a vast area, although they had neither the means nor the knowledge necessary for such a demanding task: factors and merchants were called to administer a territory they barely knew, dealing with a culture they hardly understood. The Moghul system of land revenue had broken down and, in this respect, several questions arose. Who were the owners of the land? What would the procedure be for assessing its value and the rents to be collected?

A period of corruption and mismanagement began. With the decline of agriculture and the stagnation of industry and trade, Bengal entered a phase of severe economic recession. Moreover, at the end of 1768, warning signs of a natural calamity appeared. A prolonged drought culminated in the Bengal famine of 1770, "one of the greatest catastrophes of the eighteenth century and, indeed, of modern times" (Arnold 1999: 86). It whipped out, it was said, one third of the population – perhaps even more.

Charles Grant, a future chairman of the East India Company whose first stay in Bengal took place between 1768 and 1771, was a direct witness to the calamity. This turned out to be an unexpected pretext for considerations about the Indian character: "the natives indolent, improvident, fatalists, and exposed till of late to be taxed in proportion to the produced they raised (…), had never adopted the practice of keeping a stock of grain in case of dearth" (1797: 17). Droughts and famine were "a visitation of Heaven" (*ibid:* 20), "one of those severe inflictions of the Almighty, by which offending creatures who forget their Maker, are reminded of his being, and of his government of the universe" (*ibid.*: 22).

This state of affairs required a resolute intervention of the Company: a new economic policy would be necessary. The introduction of private property – which was supposed to put an end to the indeterminacy hovering over the revenue collection system – was widely discussed.

Private property was the central theme of a typically European debate of the time, revolving around speculations about the birth of civil society. This implied different views on government and social forms, on natural and social equality or inequality, on freedom and slavery.

John Locke had seen private property as a natural right, the state of nature being defined by him as a condition of "freedom and equality" (*Second Treatise*, II, § 7). The need to safeguard such rights would have been the reason for the emergence of civil society: "no political society", he had written, would have survived "without having in itself the power to preserve the property" (VII, § 87). Only the advent of a *political or civil society* by tacit consent had been able to protect the rights and privileges inherent in the state of nature, the government having "no other end but the preservation of property" (*ibid.*: § 94).

Later perspectives differed widely regarding the reasons for and effects of the end of the state of nature. While Locke had argued that in civil society men "are left as they were in the liberty of the state of nature" (*ibid.*: § 95), Montesquieu evoked a radical break: "In the state of nature, (…) all men are born equal, but they cannot continue in this equality. Society makes them lose it, and they recover it only by the protection of the laws" (*The Spirit of Laws*, VIII, § 3). Freedom and property were therefore no longer inseparable: "As men have given up their natural independence to live under political laws, they have given up the natural community of goods to live under civil laws. By the first, they acquired liberty, by the second, property" (*ibid.*: XXVI, 15).

Rousseau had yet another point of view: the beginning of civil society could be assimilated to the claim of a land right, the origin of a whole train of misfortunes: the first man who had enclosed a plot of land, proclaiming an exclusive entitlement over it, had been the founder of civil society (*Discourse on the Origin and Foundations of Inequality Among Men,* II, 1). Social inequality and other kinds of adversities had followed.

Private property and inequality would soon be linked again by authors for whom the latter was one of the dominant principles of order. This was notably the case for François Quesnay, leader of the Physiocrat movement, whose Economic Table was published shortly after Rousseau's *Discourse on Inequality*. Like Locke, Quesnay argued that the right to private property went back to the state of nature coexisting, however, with inequality. He believed that the faculties of the body and the intellect differed from one individual to another, a divine design inaccessible to human understanding. Property was now considered incompatible with egalitarianism. Men had always had unequal rights, and civil societies would not have emerged if such differences had been abolished. Laws intended to encourage the development of social life could only ensure respect for inequality. Different approaches to private property thus led to incompatible conceptions of society.

Property played a central role in the European conjectures on the economic reform of Bengal, after the famine of 1770. Alexander Dow, a Lieutenant-Colonel of the East India Company, attributed the economic depression of Bengal to the inefficient methods of leasing land adopted by the British. He recommended the gradual sale of all lands in Bengal and Bihar by the Company. Although he did not subscribe to physiocratic principles, he emphasized the exceptional potential of Bengal for agricultural exploration, the main support of industry and commerce. Private property was a first condition: "An established idea of property", he pointed out, "is the source of all industry among individuals, and, of course, the foundation of public prosperity. When mankind are restrained from possessing any thing which they can call their own, they are but passengers in their native country" (1772: cxviii). He thought that the evils that afflicted the region would instantly disappear. The farmers would withdraw all possible benefit from their own land; and because they would be protected from that point on against the greed and arbitrariness of the collectors, they would regularly pay the stipulated taxes. Dow's essay promised "recreation": "The whole face of the country would be changed in a few years: in the place of straggling towns, composed of miserable huts, half of which are washed away every season by the rain, great and opulent cities would arise (*ibid.*: cxx).

Particular perspectives on social order loomed behind these considerations. Locke's theses on private property were, of course, an implicit reference. But freedom (as conceived by him in the past and then accepted by the Physiocrats) was a source of apprehension: "men of speculation may suppose, that the security of property to the natives might infuse a spirit of freedom, dangerous to our power, into our Indian subjects" (*ibid.*). Such fears had to be put aside. To dispel them, Dow turned to Montesquieu's well-known theory of climate: "Nature herself seems to have denied liberty to the inhabitants of the torrid zone" (*ibid.*). Granting them freedom would be "beyond the power of political arrangement" (*ibid.*), because everything – their religion, their institutions, their manners – drove them to obedience: "To give them property would only bind them with stronger ties to our interest; and make them more our subjects; or, if the British nation prefers the name – more our slaves" (*ibid.*).

Slavery had been condemned by Locke, as "so vile and miserable an estate of man, and so directly opposite to the generous temper and courage of our nation; that 'tis hardly to be conceived, that an *Englishman*, much less a gentleman, should plead for't" (*First Treatise*, I, 1). Montesquieu himself had addressed the question:

> *The state of slavery is in its own nature bad. It is neither useful to the master nor to the slave; not to the slave, because he can do nothing through a motive of virtue; nor to the master, because by having an unlimited authority over his slaves he insensibly accustoms himself to the want of all moral virtues, and thence becomes fierce, hasty, severe, choleric, voluptuous, and cruel* (The Spirit of Laws, XV, 1).

This was not Montesquieu's only point of view on the subject: "There are countries where the excess of heat enervates the body, and renders men so slothful and dispirited that nothing but the fear of chastisement can oblige them to perform any laborious duty: slavery is there more reconcilable with reason" (*ibid.*: XV: 7). But the philosopher seemed to hesitate: "as all men are born equal, slavery must be accounted unnatural, though in some countries it be founded on natural reason" (*ibid.*). Dow adopted the opinion best suited to his own thesis.

II

In 1773, an institutional link was introduced between the Crown and the East India Company. Warren Hastings, who had joined the Company as early as 1750, was appointed Governor-General and controlled the Presidencies of Madras and Bombay. His authority was limited by a Supreme Council whose members did not owe any allegiance to the Company.

Revenue taxation continued to require a solution, and Philip Francis, one of the Councillors, was sure he had something to contribute. Arriving in Calcutta in 1774, he had no direct experience of local realities; the reform he had in mind rested on the principles of Physiocratic economic theory. Land property was its foundation. But, again, to whom did the land belong? The question stemmed from European premises. Francis arbitrarily assumed – or pretended to have assumed – that private ownership of land had prevailed in India before British rule. He claimed that the rights of the Zamindars, ancient collectors of revenue under Moghul authority, had long been established and intended to give them the privileges they were supposed to have lost. Having apparently in mind "the old feudal maxim *nulle terre sans seigneur*", he seemed to believe that "for every plot of land, large or small, in Bengal there must be an owner, and that every subordinate cultivator on the soil must be there by virtue of a contract" (Firminger 1917, I: cccviii). Invested "with characteristics he had never possessed" (Weitzman 1929: 82), the Zamindar was seen as a replica of the "gentleman-farmer" – the "central figure in the English agrarian scene at this time" (Guha 1996 [1963]: 108) – "the transmission-belt helping economic power and political authority to circulate in society" (*ibid.*: 114). In fact, Francis had no definitive ideas as to the allocation of property rights over the land. Just a few months before completing his Plan for a Settlement of the Revenues of Bengal, Bihar, and Orissa, Guha observed, he still admitted that land ownership could be attributed not only to Zamindars but also to Talukdars and even to peasants. Describing the Zamindars as members of a decaying aristocracy "sunk into a state of Sloth, Stupidity, Beggary and Contempt", he wondered whether they should "really be chosen to lead the coming agrarian resurgence in the country" (*ibid.*: 126). Francis' Plan was initially rejected but later adopted by Lord Cornwallis, who succeeded Hastings as Governor-General.

Hastings returned to England in 1785, not without having given his full support to William Jones regarding the foundation of the Asiatic Society of Bengal in 1784. Jones had arrived in Calcutta in 1783 to take up office as a judge in the High Court of Bengal. His extraordinary linguistic skills earned him a well-deserved academic reputation. He certainly did not escape the constraints imposed by his culture and personal convictions, but this should not minimize the importance of the role he played. The novelty of his perspectives, like those of some of his colleagues at the Asiatic Society, is best assessed by comparing them with what was generally admitted at the time. As Hastings observed in his "Introduction" to the *Bhagavad-Gita*, recently translated by Charles Wilkins, "[i]t is not very long since the inhabitants of India were considered by many, as creatures scarce elevated above the degree of savage life; nor, I fear, is that prejudice yet wholly eradicated" (1785: 13).

***

Lord Cornwallis was appointed Governor-General in 1786. He had no real knowledge of India but strived "to make everything as English as possible in a country which resembles England in nothing" (in Aspinall 1931: 173). One of the reforms he was determined to introduce was Francis' system of perpetual land ownership: "The security of property (…) and the certainty which each individual will now feel of being allowed to enjoy the fruits of his own labours, must operate uniformly as incitements to exertion and industry" (in Ross 1859, I: 553). He believed that the permanent revenue settlement would stabilize the economic situation of the Zamindars, thereby limiting their proverbial coercion over the cultivators. It would ultimately be a source of "wealth and happiness", an effective tool for creating a harmonious social organization. Only then could there be an establishment of a "regular gradation of ranks (…) which is nowhere more necessary than in this country for preserving order in civil society" (*ibid.*: 554).

The more the apologists of Westernization insisted on the pre-eminence of the European model of order, the greater was the emphasis on the disarray of Indian society. Such was the spirit of Grant's project. Upon his return to India in 1774, he was appointed Secretary of the Board of Trade in Calcutta, an organization that would become of the utmost importance in Cornwallis' strategy. The experience he acquired while engaged in the Company's commercial activities made him an indispensable collaborator of the Governor-General, allowing his active participation in the establishment of the permanent settlement. He considered that his competence was based on solid knowledge of local realities: he did not think he was running the risk of being led astray by "conjectural, hypothetical reasonings" (Embree 1962: 113).

Nothing could justify such self-assurance. At the end of the 18th century, European contact with the country remained superficial. Henry Thomas Colebrooke regretted not finding in India anything comparable to the records of civil data used in Europe as major information tools: "no bills of mortality, nor registers of births, marriages, and burials, afford data for calculation" (1804: 13). To assess the number of inhabitants in a village or region the British often had to resort to indirect expedients, such as the consumption of staple foods. Given the obstacles to communication, one might be surprised by Grant's claims of proficiency, that were based on the fact that he had spent "many years in India, and a considerable portion of them in the interior of our provinces, inhabited almost entirely by natives (…)" (1797: 43). His opinions seemed to have been forged to support Cornwallis' perspectives: India desperately needed European conceptions of order. Grant's *Observations* were a counterpoint to the testimony of the Orientalists: "It has suited the views of some philosophers to represent [the people of India] as amiable and respectable". He thought this was sharply contradicted by what "the natives themselves freely acknowledge of each other (…), they are a people exceedingly depraved" (*ibid.*).

Grant believed that Bengalis lacked all the basic rules of social life: "the practice of cheating, pilfering, tricking, and imposing, in the ordinary transactions of life" were common among them (*ibid.*: 44); "frauds, deceptions, evasions, and procrastinations, in every line of life, in all professions, perpetually occur" (*ibid.*: 45). This was so deeply imprinted in their character that the measures taken by the Governor-General seemed partially doomed to failure: "although the legal reforms introduced by Lord Cornwallis will purify, it may be hoped, the fountains of justice, yet the best administration of law will not eradicate the internal principles of depravity" (*ibid.*: 47).

The absence of the "primary virtues of society" was emphasized with linguistic versality: "dastardly" and "unprincipled", the inhabitants of the "lower provinces" sought "their ends by mean artifices, low cunning, intrigue, falsehood, servility, and hypocritical obsequiousness" (*ibid.*); "discord, hatred, abuse, slanders, injuries, complaints, and litigations, (…) prevail to a surprising degree" (*ibid.*); "the deliberate malice, the falsehood, the calumnies, and the avowed enmity with which [they] pursue each other, and sometimes from father to son, offer a very mortifying view of the human character" (*ibid.*: 47-8).

The author wondered: "Are we pledged to support, for all generations, by the authority of our government and the power of our arms, the miseries which ignorance and knavery have so long entailed upon a large portion of the human race?" (*ibid.*: 146-47). The answer was implicit in the question. Grant's main goal was to find the means to put an end to the chaos raging "among our Asiatic subjects, [destroying] their happiness, and [preventing] every species of improvement" (*ibid.*: 146). Westernization became the path to follow: "the communication of our light and knowledge to [the Indians], would prove the best remedy for their disorders" (*ibid.*: 148). Learning the English language would allow access to "our useful literature", an effective way of making clear "the great use we make of reason on all subjects, and in all affairs" (*ibid.*: 152). Through this medium, Indians could become progressively acquainted "with the simple elements of our arts, our philosophy and religion. These acquisitions would silently undermine, and at length subvert, the fabric of error" (*ibid.*: 149). Step by step, Indians would ultimately cease to be Indians:

> *[T]he general mass of their opinions would be rectified; and above all, they would see a better system of principles and morals. New views of duty as rational creatures would open upon them; and that mental bondage in which they have long been holden, would gradually dissolve* (ibid.: 152).

Grant admitted for a moment the "idle, visionary, and absurd" character of his project; but, on second thoughts, he considered it "unwarrantable to infer, that because the Hindoos, (...) are at present low in their sentiments, conduct, and aims, they must always remain so" (*ibid.*: 155).

Starting from these premises, several texts of the period attempted to re-think, re-found or re-create India. The underlying model corresponded to Cornwallis' vision – that of a society structured by a "regular gradation of ranks", the Anglican model of hierarchy. Human society was then conceived as "a hierarchy because the whole of Creation was a yet more vast hierarchy, reaching down from God to the lowest form of life. It was an idea familiar to us as the 'great chain of being'" (Clark 2000: 166). This grandiose and largely abstract scheme was hardly applicable to India. It was, however, the only means available to Europeans to approach a reality whose contours escaped them. Their efforts would inevitably be doomed to failure. If, at one point, the Abbé Dubois imagined a hierarchy of Shudra castes, he immediately recognized that "the natives themselves" did not agree in any way to their relative positions…

***

The census operations, developed by the East India Company since the first decades of the 19th century, provided some of the information considered essential to the administration of the territory: "One of the chief utilities of a correct Census", James Prinsep pointed out, "is that it introduces a right understanding as to what should be the produce of any tax levied upon the food, the houses, or the inhabitants of a Town" (1832: 480). The census he conducted on the town of Benares gathered information about the number and size of houses, the number of inhabitants distinguished by sex, age and religion, and occupations distributed by *varnas*, plus Hindu Fakirs and Muslims.

For decades, there was no appreciable progress in the acquisition of further details. Elementary concepts were summarily formulated, the basic principles of Hindu society remaining incomprehensible. As in the time of Dubois, the European observers were in a quandary. Only the idea of an *order* of precedence occurred to them, but it barely helped to envision a reality which still appeared to them as *chaos*.

The Indian Revolt of 1857/58 dictated the end of the East India Company and the inception of the rule of the British Crown. New conceptions were then introduced regarding the purpose of census operations and the organization of their findings. The *Census of England and Wales for 1861* adopted completely new classification methods, immediately transposed to the Indian context. In 1871/ 72, an attempt was made to obtain the first statistical survey for the whole of British India, concerning age, caste, religion, education and infirmities. This paved the way for a broader vision of Indian society by Europeans, although its organizing principles remained obscure. As someone observed at the turn of the last quarter of the 19th century, piercing the meaning of the caste system would have required "a life-time of labor" – and no "scientific" research on the topic had been carried out so far. On the contrary, "the attempts of European writers (...) [had] generally tended to make confusion worse confounded" (Cornish 1874: 116).

III

An overview of the immense ethnographic diversity of Bengal had been provided in 1872 by Edward Tuite Dalton. But the need for scientific reflection was required, as Herbert Hope Risley strongly emphasized: "Ethnological work in India has been done almost entirely by Government officers, and it must be confessed that Indian official literature is not exactly attractive reading" (1886: 71). Risley's critical remarks on the subject were taken up even more vigorously shortly afterwards:

> *[T]he ethnographical data to be found in Indian official reports are, as a rule, neither full enough nor precise enough to appeal very strongly to European ethnologists. Such reports, moreover, are not readily accessible to students; their titles give a very slight clue to the nature of their contents; and any information regarding custom which they contain is generally buried under a mass of highly technical and uninteresting*

> *matter. Clearly it is not to be expected that writers on general ethnology should toil through this mountain of chaff in the hope of picking out the scattered grains of knowledge which it might contain* (1891 a: 237).

***

In 1885, Risley had been commissioned to lead an ethnographic survey of Bengal, an opportunity to introduce in India the methods of "scientific anthropometry". This coincided with the publication of Paul Topinard's *Éléments d'Anthropologie Générale,* a book which exerted a very decisive influence on Risley. Topinard's objective was to achieve a classification of human groups according to their physical characteristics. Applied to the Hindu social system, this approach was supposed to establish an unquestionable relationship between the position of each caste in a *presumed* social hierarchy and physical features, previously measured and scaled. The ancient European perspective on social precedence could finally be validated by science. In short, the universe of castes was converted into a rigorously defined system, made up of elements whose positions were determined by mathematical calculations. Such views were the subject of criticism, but this was stubbornly ignored by Risley.

Having been appointed Census Commissioner for 1901, he carried out large-scale research with the help of his provincial census superintendents. His aim was to confirm, through "native public opinion", the hierarchical arrangement of castes. Developed over a short period of time, the census operations necessarily excluded systematic anthropometric measurements. It was for this reason – not because Risley abandoned his previous views, as recently suggested by C. J. Fuller[1] – that anthropometry could not then be used as an analytical instrument.

1. Fuller 2024. We will return to this question in Chapter Six.

Most of Risley's superintendents repeatedly noted that public opinion concerning a (putative) caste hierarchy was totally untrustworthy. The remarks of E. A. Gait, one of his closest collaborators, would have required particular attention: the Hindus, he had written, were "strangely indifferent" to the social status of castes which were not in direct contact with theirs. Unconcerned about the obvious implications of this observation, Risley continued to defend the consistency of his own views.

Despite his unshakeable conviction in the success of his methods and conclusions, Risley never abandoned the idea that hierarchy coexisted with ... anarchy. As far back as in Buddha's time, he maintained, the *varna* system was nothing but a theoretical arrangement that was in sharp contrast to the *chaotic* fragmentation of castes: "Then, as now, Indian society was made up of a medley of diverse and heterogeneous groups" (1915 [1908]: 260). *Then as now...*

Simultaneously affirming the hierarchy of castes and their disorderly fragmentation, Risley tacitly admitted his incomprehension. The same misunderstanding was expressed by Gait, in his general report on the Census of 1911: "The segmentation of Hindu society is much more complicated than appears at first sight". He regretted the "vague ideas of the subject on the part of the people themselves", stressing again their "indifference to social distinctions with which they are not directly concerned" (1913: 365). He was incapable of grasping the contours of a system which had "grown up gradually without any set design or purpose" (*ibid.*: 366). The proclaimed hierarchy had not substituted the persistent feeling of chaos with a form of intelligibility. Nevertheless, the importance of the concept in "our understanding of ethnographic realities" continued to be asserted and is still strongly underlined by Knut M. Rio and Olaf H. Smedal in their introduction to *Hierarchy. Persistence and Transformation in Social Formations* (2009: 1).

Risley's caste hierarchy, despite the controversial circumstances of its emergence, has been incorporated into and "normalized" by sociological and anthropological knowledge. Significantly, the marks of its problematic origin were never erased. Hindu society is often characterized as *undoubtedly hierarchical*. Yet caste hierarchy has been declared "uncertain and arguable" (Srinivas),[2] "unstable" (Stevenson), [3] "ambiguous" and "fluid" (Mayer),[4] "floating" (*flottante*) (Dumont),[5] "flexible" and "loose" (Fuller),[6] "revolving" (*hiérarchie tournante*) (Malamoud),[7] "inconsistent" and "muddled" (Gupta).[8] Such attributes ruin the notion to which they apply: arguable, ambiguous, unstable, revolving "hierarchies" cannot in any way be seen as hierarchies.

---

2. Srinivas 1952, 1955.
3. Stevenson 1954.
4. Mayer 1960.
5. Dumont 1957, 1966.
6. Fuller 1976.
7. Malamoud 1989.
8. Gupta 2000.

CHAPTER-2

A LEGACY OF THE AGE OF ENLIGHTENMENT

I

The French Jesuit Gaston-Laurent Coeurdoux arrived in South India in 1732, where he developed intense missionary work. He is the author of a lost manuscript partially preserved, as Sylvia Murr has shown, in two different texts which do not completely overlap (Murr 1987 b: 41).

One of those texts – undoubtedly the result of extensive borrowing, probably reworked – is the well-known *Moeurs, institutions et cérémonies des peuples de l'Inde* by the Abbé Jean-Antoine Dubois. Considered a repository of useful information for the servants of the East India Company, the manuscript was acquired in 1808 by Lord William Bentinck, future Governor-General of India. An English translation appeared in 1817 under the title *Description of the Character, Manners and Customs of the People of India, and of Their Institutions, Religious and Civil*. A second text, *Moeurs et coutumes des Indiens*, apparently an abridged version of the original, was completed in 1776-1777 by Nicolas-Jacques Desvaulx, perhaps with the collaboration of Coeurdoux himself.

Murr sees in *Moeurs et coutumes des Indiens* a synthesis of different levels of meaning. In addition to its apologetic purpose, the work aimed to promote "Indianism as a scientific discipline" (*ibid.:* 79). It is not clear how apologetic and scientific concerns may coexist, but we will not dwell on this aspect of her interpretation. It is relevant, however, to discuss the argument according to which a pedagogical comparison had been tacitly intended by Coeurdoux. Murr claims that he had idealized a society in which temporal power was subordinated to spiritual power. Based on the hierarchy of endogamous groups, with Brahmins at the top, Indian society had been presented as a model by the Jesuit (*ibid.*: 154). "What a fascinating example for Europe!", she exclaims (*ibid.*: 155, our translation). India would have achieved, more perfectly than France, a universal ideal: "the permanence of the established order" (*ibid.*). Brahmins were an example (*ibid.*: 156). They had certainly plunged into idolatry but even this deserved consideration: India had remained faithful to the ideal of a "perfect order in spite of the fact that she had gone astray into the 'darkness' of paganism" (*ibid.*: 159, our translation).

The Jesuit's perspectives were supposed to be steeped in empathetic feelings: "Being the noblest by blood and the most polite by manners, the brahmins embody (...) the Indian nobility", representing the quintessence of Indian civilization (*ibid.*: 158, our translation). The transparency of social relationships in their villages – where "no one can hide his life from the gaze of others" – could only arouse sympathy: the Jesuit professed a secret admiration for their communities whose rules evoked to him those of Christian monastic orders... (*ibid.*: 156).

This is an untenable stretch of the imagination. Nowhere did Coeurdoux glorify the Brahmins – which, of course, would have proved contrary to the purpose of missionary action. The members of the Hindu priestly class were, for him, anything but paragons of virtue... All Indians, he asserted, were skilled in the art of disguising the truth; Brahmins, however, surpassed everyone in this respect (in Murr a: 74). In order to know them better, a careful examination of their customs was necessary, although the author warned his readers that the outcome of such an exercise could not be advantageous for them (*ibid.*: 75).

Moeurs et coutumes des Indiens in no way praises the caste system. Murr's interpretation is just an expression of the common perspective according to which any discourse on India necessarily presupposes hierarchy. Coeurdoux certainly admitted that relations of "subordination" – inherent in the original *varna* model – had existed in a *distant past*. As he pointed out from the beginning of his work, nothing seemed more ancient than the four *varnas* ("main tribes" or "general castes" in his terminology) – which were said to emanate from the body of the Supreme Being: Brahmins from his face; Rajputs from his shoulders; Vaishyas from his belly; Shudras from his feet (*ibid.*: 14). This was an allegory alluding not only to the rigorous ranking of the *varnas* but also to the tasks assigned to their members (*ibid.*).[1] Such organization, however, had long since been replaced, the new one composed of a large number of groups that did not comply with the ancient rules.

***

Coeurdoux's arguments were shared by the majority of his European contemporaries: the history of India was conceived as a chapter in the history of the world, viewed in the light of the Biblical tradition. The golden age of the past was over when the corruption and wickedness of men spread across the earth. The Flood caused the fall of humanity into the earliest stage of civilization, and a new period started with the strenuousness of each new beginning. In Pufendorf's words, "the Root of the Evil"

1. The RgVeda (X, 90) describes how the representatives of the four varnas were born from Purusha (one of the Vedic names of the Creator). Brahma – instead of Purusha – is the god mentioned in the version to which the Jesuit had access.

which had manifested itself before the Flood had not entirely disappeared afterwards: "as no human Affairs come immediately to Perfection, so were the first Institutions of Civil Society very simple and imperfect" (1719 [1695], I, § 3).

Indian civilization, as described by certain Europeans of the 18th century, bore the marks of the new start. The memory of the past had not been completely lost: "the first founders of the Indian nations, sons or grand-sons of Noah (…), had brought with them the knowledge of the true God" (in Murr 1987 a: 125, our translation). If the Brahmins of the present wished to preserve their teachings, "they would retire to their villages", devoting themselves to reading and studying. But "such a philosophical life" no longer suited their ambition (*ibid.*: 73). They had moved away from the old wisdom; they had spread superstition and idolatry, obscuring the "purest ideas of natural religion" (*ibid.*: 111).

With the fading of old religious conceptions, society itself was reshaped. Along with "the seven famous penitents of India", a great man named Manourou – Noah, perhaps! – survived the cataclysm and divided the Indian people into various castes (*ibid.*: 14-15). These are the groups – *jatis* – that exist "at the present day", Dubois explained (1906 [1897]: 48). Caste distinctions, he underlined, were "probably (…) common to the majority of ancient nations", because the legislators of the past had perceived that this was the most convenient solution for "nations in an embryonic stage" (*ibid.*: 32).

The *varnas* – of which the *jatis* were believed to be subdivisions – had reappeared, but the old principle of "subordination" was no longer respected: although the Brahmins still occupied the highest position, in some parts of the country their prerogatives were challenged, even by people with a low status. Some of them were "rich merchants" who indulged in tasks formerly carried out by Vaishyas. They also engaged in agriculture, while Shudras occasionally devoted themselves to writing. Equally strange for the Jesuit was the fact that he had never seen Vaishyas claiming superiority over the Shudras: "I have never seen the merchants put themselves above the Choutres [Shudras], most of whom would not accept, for anything in the world, to drink a glass of water in the house of a Chetti or Cometti" (in Murr 1987 a: 7, our translation). Granting the Vaishyas the third position in the *varna* system, he was just reproducing, he explained, the traditional ranking found in ancient books.

Because the old four-group distinction had broken down into a wide variety of social units, fragmentation – rather than a "chain of subordination" – was now prevalent:

Golden age	**Post-Flood society**
Knowledge of the true God	Superstition
Social perfection	Fall into an "embryonic" social stage
Cohesion: well-defined classes (*varnas*) hierarchically arranged	Fragmentation: a multiplicity of castes (*jatis*) ignoring the old hierarchical order
Precise functions assigned to each class	Uncertainty as to the functions assigned to each group

Table 1: *Past and present social structure according to Coeurdoux (Desvaulx's version and Dubois).*

II

Fragmentation was a first step towards a new order: "the more classes and distinctions are instituted, the easier it will be to govern society and keep morality", the Jesuit claimed (*ibid.*: 8, our translation). But India, he immediately clarified, was not an example of good governance. The country's imperfect political structure was further proof of the weakness of a rudimentary state of civilization.

The Hindu Sovereign portrayed by Coeurdoux was deprived of the ability to fulfil his functions. Greedy and neglectful, he was unable to ensure "good manners" among the people. Such a lack of commitment to public affairs, Dubois observed, was common to his whole class: "the princes and the aristocracy live in extreme indolence, attaching little importance to making their dependents happy" (1906: 33).

Who, then, could maintain social stability? In Coeurdoux's words, "there is no other resource to keep some order than the authority of castes". They uphold "morality and repress vices"; they alone provide safety, preventing an often-evoked risk: the return to barbarism (in Murr 1987 a: 8).

Which castes were endowed with such power? There is no mention of specific groups. The particular identity of this or that caste did not seem important; all the Jesuit emphasized was the set of skills included under the same designation: "arts". Dubois expressed himself in similar terms. Speaking of "castes" in general, he actually alluded to their safeguarding of "arts and sciences". Taking the part for the whole, the author was convinced that "it is simply and solely due to the distribution of the people into castes that India did not lapse into a state of barbarism, and that she preserved and perfected the arts and sciences of civilization" (1906: 28).

A sharp opposition was thus postulated between groups promoting "arts and sciences" – the very spirit of civilization – and sovereigns who, inhibiting their development, were seen as obstacles to progress: only by protecting themselves from the greediness of the latter could the former "preserve and improve" their expertise (Coeurdoux in Murr 1978 a: 9). Situations had been reported where the abuses of Princes, their despotism and arbitrariness, were discouraged by caste authority. Some castes were known for their firmness even when confronted with "small insults" or "slight extortions" perpetrated by Princes: such was the force of a right consecrated by custom.

This narrative did not match the observed reality. What, then, could have been the inspiration for the Jesuit's account?

***

The hostility between Craftsmen and Rulers was a central theme of contemporary European theories regarding the birth of civil society. Coeurdoux did not explicitly reveal his sources but they were familiar to most Western readers.

A tension between "arts and sciences" and "political power" was often evoked – albeit from different perspectives – by the contractualist theorists of the 17th and 18th centuries. Hobbes had claimed in 1651 that a decisive role was played by political power in the birth of civil society. In the state of nature, he imagined, "there is no place for Industry; because the fruit thereof is uncertain; and consequently no Culture of the Earth (…); no Arts; no Letters; no Society" (*Leviathan* I: xiii). Self-interest prevailed and the war of all against all became widespread. Only a government based on mutual consent could ensure lasting peace: "It may peradventure be thought", he conceded, "there was never such a time, nor condition of warre as this; and I believe it was never generally so, over all the world, but there are many places, where they live so now". An example was found among "the savage people of *America* (who) have no government at all; and live at this day in [a] brutish manner" (*ibid.*). This was held to be sufficient proof of the accuracy of *Leviathan*'s theory: if such societies existed in close proximity to the state of nature, only the absence of political power accounted for their rudimentary condition.

Pufendorf questioned these views. In his opinion, it was not political power but arts and sciences that represented the decisive force in the emergence of civil society. Of course, man in the state of nature was still ignorant of "all the various Arts and Improvements" (1729 [1672], II, ii, §1). Nature, however, had propelled him towards civil society, pre-defining in some way the traits of his singularity: "A Horse has the natural Faculty of prancing, which an Ass has not; a Parrot of prating; a Field of bearing Corn, and a Hill Vines; a Man of discoursing, and of learning divers Arts and Sciences" (*ibid.*, VII, i, § 3).

A shift had occurred. Social stability and well-being depended after all on the development of arts and sciences, and the Rulers themselves were invited to exercise self-restraint – warned not to confuse "their own interest with the real interest of the State" (1719 [1695]).

In an Essay published in 1742, Hume, for his part, pointed out that "it is impossible for the arts and sciences to arise, at first, among any people unless that people enjoy the blessing of a free government" (1889: 177). He stated that

> *[i]n the first ages of the world, when men are as yet barbarous and ignorant, they seek no farther security against mutual violence and injustice, than the choice of some rulers, few or many, in whom they place an implicit confidence, without providing any security, by laws or political institutions, against the violence of these rulers* (ibid.: 178).

This paved the way to arbitrary power, the sovereign governing "the subjects with full authority, as if they were his own; and with negligence or tyranny, as belonging to another". Hence, "to expect (…) that the arts and sciences should take their first rise in a monarchy, is to expect a contradiction", for "a barbarous policy debases the people, and for ever prevents all improvements" (*ibid.*: 179).

Coeurdoux's reflection on Indian society was in part an attempt to reorganize some of the major themes of this European debate.[2] India was seen as an embryonic society, living in a state of precarious equilibrium between opposing forces: on the one hand, arts and sciences, an expression of natural faculties, impelling men towards perfection (Pufendorf); on the other, the arbitrariness and despotism of political Rulers, enemies of progress (Hume). But, regarding one particular aspect at least, Hume's perspectives needed to be reconsidered: castes devoted to the exercise of arts and sciences were in no way deprived of laws and regulations. They were invested of an authority which had developed despite the Rulers and therefore independently of their tyranny.

III

Of course, the Hindu social world was not reducible to a conflictual coexistence of Artisans and Sovereigns: they were not, according to Coeurdoux, the only social actors whose relationship evoked the transition to civil society.

Man in the state of nature had been portrayed by Hobbes as a helpless and fearful being, incessantly at the mercy of violent

---

2. The importance attributed to the relation of arts and sciences to morals had been the topic chosen by the Academy of Dijon for its *concours académique* of 1749. The prize had been awarded to Rousseau's first *Discourse*, a text stressing the tension between civilization and barbarism. His thesis was opposed to the views which had been previously adopted: arts and sciences were now a source of corruption and unhappiness. Rousseau took up the question in his *Second Discourse*: only the arts not requiring "the collaboration of several hands" allowed men to live "free, healthy, good and happy" (1997: 167). That could not have been the case regarding metallurgy and agriculture; these arts, by reinforcing the rights of property, "ruined Mankind" (*ibid.*: 168). Another cause of the misfortune inherent in the emergence of civil society was the imperfection of government. The relation between the arts and political power in Rousseau's work still reflected the centrality of a classical debate.

death; his life was "solitary, poore, nasty, brutish, and short" (*Leviathan* I: xiii). Pufendorf imagined him "thrown at a Venture into the World", completely abandoned to himself – "naked, able to utter nothing but an inarticulate Sound, a Stranger to all Institution and Discipline, amazed and startled at the Things about him, and even at his own Being". Food deprivation "would make him seize greedily on any Thing that was near him, his Thirst would direct him to the first Water, and Dens or Trees would afford a Refuge from the Injuries of Weather" (1729, II, ii, § 2).

Such appeared to be the condition of the Untouchables, who lived in the "greatest disorder", had "neither education nor principles of honor" (Coeurdoux in Murr 1987 a: 172), competed "for carrion with dogs and crows" (*ibid.*) and were regarded therefore "more or less as animals" (*ibid.*: 173). Some slept "in the branches of the thickest-foliaged trees", without any "communication whatever with the rest of the world" (Dubois 1906: 61). They evoked the ever-present danger of savage life, some of them being "looked upon as almost another race of beings altogether outside the pale of society" (*ibid.*: 49).

The Abbé concluded that "a State consisting entirely of such inhabitants could not long endure, and could not fail to lapse before long into a condition of barbarism"; it would be a nation "worse than the hordes of cannibals who wander in the vast waste of Africa, and would soon take to devouring each other" (*ibid.*: 29). Here too, the institution of caste prevented the return to barbarism:

> *We can picture what would become of the Hindus if they were not kept within the bounds of duty by the rules and penalties of caste, by looking at the position of the Pariahs, or outcastes of India, who, checked by no moral restraint, abandon themselves to their natural propensities* (ibid.).

The term "caste" is employed here again in a restrictive sense. Although contextually designated as "castes" – the "Pariah's caste" is referred to by Dubois – the Untouchables did not seem to have abandoned the state of nature. They would have driven the country towards anarchy were it not for the providential role of the Artisans.

The Brahmins themselves were blamed for reprehensible behaviour that was only partially corrected by the institution of caste. In the Jesuit's words, their malevolence, comparable to the Untouchables' rudeness (in Murr 1987 a: 172), was implicitly depicted as an expression of dominant attitudes characterizing the emergence of civil society.

When men broke free from their loneliness and came closer to each other, we are told in Rousseau's *Second Discourse*, "everyone began to look at everyone else and to wish to be looked at himself". Then, "public esteem acquired a price": each one tried to assert a particular talent or skill, and "this was the first step to inequality and vice" (1997: 166). Men had suddenly begun to value "qualities that could attract consideration" – whether they really possessed them or just pretended that they did: "To be and to appear became two entirely different things, and from this distinction arose ostentatious display, deceitful cunning, and all the vices that follow in their wake" (*ibid.*: 170).

This fitted the Jesuit's perspective on the Brahmins; he believed they were supreme masters in the art of lying (in Murr 1987 a: 74). Only appearance mattered to them; in order to obtain public consideration, they felt no reluctance to show themselves other than they really were. They acknowledged the unreasonable nature of their practices but did not abandon them, fearing to be despised. Transgressions occurred, however, when they were certain they were not being observed (*ibid.*: 67). Long prayers tended to be cut short; cumbersome rituals were not always respected. Inside their villages (*agraharas*), social pressure was inevitable. Because they were constantly in front of each other (*sous les yeux les uns des autres*), they pretended to comply with the rules. But only fear of contempt and material considerations led them to act in that way. Their duplicity was well known, hence, the common saying: "Full Brahmin within the *agrahara*; half-Brahmin seen from afar; Shudra if completely lost from sight" (*ibid.*: 68)...

The current low standing of Brahmins' behaviour illustrated the decay of the values instituted by ancient legislators. This had been foreseen. The old lawmakers knew perfectly well that, over the course of time, part of their teachings would be adulterated (Dubois 1906: 30). Brahmins were responsible for unacceptable changes: "I cannot believe", the Abbé declared, "that the original lawgivers of the Hindus intended to introduce a creed so abominable as that which at present exists amongst them" (*ibid.*: 105). Desiring to endow the Hindus with "durable and inviolable rules", they had combined "in an unmistakable manner those two great foundations of orderly government, religion and politics" (*ibid.*: 30). Hence, *castes* had been endorsed with a power opposed not only to the harmful actions of Sovereigns but also to the teachings of the Brahmins themselves, thus tempering the spirit of Hinduism: "It may (...) be said that caste regulations counteract to a great extent the evil effects which would otherwise be produced on the national character by a religion that encourages the most unlicensed depravity of morals" (*ibid.*: 33). The deplorable conceptions of the Brahmins – their "absurd theogony", expressed in the "decorations of [their] temples, as in [their] dogmas and ritual" (*ibid.*) – had been severely blamed if not totally rejected... by the authority of *castes*.

Strange as it may seem, Sovereigns, Priests and Untouchables were somehow excluded from the "caste system". They represented, so to speak, conceptual boundaries of what appeared to be the central core of society:

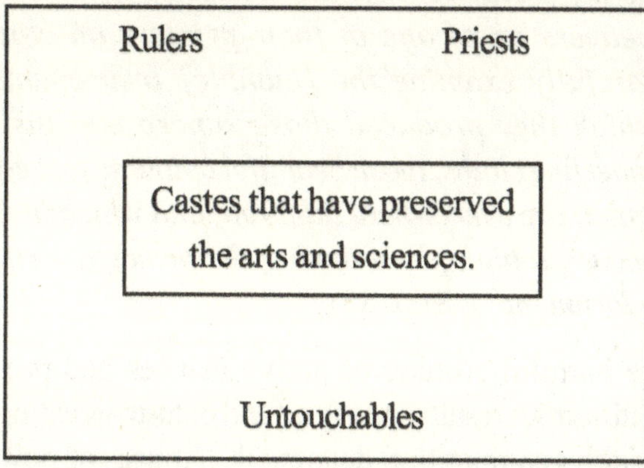

Table 2: *"Centre" and "periphery" of Indian society (Coeurdoux and Dubois).*

IV

Strict allegiance to the European conjectures about the origin of civil society implied a detachment from the "real" Hindu society. The opposition between Rulers and Artisans had no correspondence with the observed reality, which was nevertheless impossible to completely ignore: Artisans could not fail to submit to the will of Sovereigns. Contradictory points of view therefore ended up coexisting in *Moeurs et coutumes des Indiens*, the Jesuit postulating simultaneously the authority of the Craftsmen, who opposed the tyranny of the Princes (in Murr 1987 a: 8), and the tyrannical behaviour of the Princes, who hindered the success of the Craftsmen: "as soon as a worker seems to prevail over the others of his profession, he is forced to work for the Palace, where he is poorly paid" (*ibid.*: 9, our translation).

Dubois took this contradiction to extremes, the very skills of Craftsmen being both affirmed and denied. To appreciate their wonderful ability,

> *we have only to visit the workshop of one of their weavers or of one of their printers on cloth and carefully examine the [humble] instruments with which they produced those superb muslins, those superfine cloths, those beautiful coloured piece-goods, which are everywhere admired, and which in Europe occupy a high place among the principal articles of adornment"* (1906: 35).

The harmful attitude of native Princes had produced, however, disastrous results: "every art and industry is extinguished and all healthy competition deadened". Abuses of power and arbitrariness were "the chief and almost the only reason why progress in the arts has been so slow among the Hindus, and why in this respect they are now far behind other nations" (*ibid.*).

In this context, Dubois could not do more than imagine what the progress of the arts *might have been* under less adverse conditions: India "*would have reached* a high standard of perfection in [arts and industries] *had not the avarice of her rulers prevented it*"; "perfection in arts and manufactures *would undoubtedly have been attained (...) if (...) the cupidity of the [Hindu rulers] had not acted as a check* (*ibid.*: 34, italics added).

The art of carpenters, masons, goldsmiths, blacksmiths and coppersmiths was languishing, and this was also true of music, painting and sculpture. As far as music was concerned, "Hindus are no further advanced (…) now than they were two or three thousand years ago" (*ibid.:* 64). With regard to painting, "one never see anything but daubs"…

The Abbé seemed indifferent to the conflict between his own statements:

Dubois 1906: 28	**Dubois 1906: 35**
"[India] preserved and perfected the arts and sciences of civilization whilst most other nations of the earth remained in a state of barbarism".	"Progress in arts has been (...) slow among the Hindus and (...) in this respect they are now far behind other nations".

Considerations of the degradation of the arts were accompanied by a negative assessment of the social status of the Artisans themselves. Craftsmen "employed in mechanical or ornamental arts are very much looked down upon and despised" (*ibid.*: 63); "liberal arts (…) are left entirely to the lower castes of the Sudras" (*ibid.*). These lower castes were, after all, the groups who had preserved the spirit of civilization – the castes that were indispensable to the maintenance of order and to the well-being of the State…

The Jesuit used and adapted the contractualists' rhetoric with the obvious aim of devaluing the role of the dominant groups in Hindu society. The overappraisal of castes proficient in the arts and sciences was the counterpart of the discrediting of Brahmins and Sovereigns. But the fiction was not only in conflict with the observed reality. It also bore the marks of divergence between the adopted sources themselves.

It is stated at the beginning of *Moeurs et coutumes des Indiens* that "the esteem of the public makes possible to know [which castes] prevail over others and which are nearly equal" (in Murr 1987 a: 6, our translation). Those were the terms through which Pufendorf had established the criteria defining relative positions in European societies: "*Esteem* is the *Value* which is set upon Persons in common Life, according to which they may be *equall'd* or *compar'd* with others, and to be rated either *higher* or *lower* than those they are *compared* with" (1729, VIII, iv, § 1). This value was a guarantee of social order:

> *As the chief Reason why a* Price *was set upon* Things, *was, that when they were to be exchanged or removed from one Person to another, they might be the better* compared *with one another; so the End intended by* Esteem, *is, that we may be able to form a* Comparison *between Men, by setting a* Value *upon them, and, in consequence, establish a becoming* Order *and* Distance *between them, whenever they should happen to be united; it evidently appearing, that nothing was more absolutely inconsistent with the Convenience of Life, than an universal* Equality (ibid.).

As already seen, "esteem" was also evoked by Rousseau, who nevertheless conceived it as a cause of anarchy. In his description of the nascent society, each individual had endeavoured to assert real or imagined merits, thus claiming to be entitled to exclusive preferences in the eyes of others. "From these first preferences arose vanity and contempt on the one hand, shame and envy on the other" (1997: 166). And later in the text: "consuming ambition, the ardent desire to raise one's relative fortune less out of genuine need than *in order to place oneself above others*, instills in all men a black inclination to harm one another, a secret jealousy" (*ibid.*: 171, italics added). Coeurdoux accepted this standpoint too, stressing thereby Indian anarchy: "As for the particular castes (*jatis*), each individual praises his own group and places it above the others" (in Murr 1987 a: 6, our translation). He noted that, in India, "public esteem" depends on the purity attributed to each caste. The Brahmins occupied, therefore, the summit of the social structure: viewed as "cleaner than most other Indians", they enjoyed the highest public consideration. But we also have seen that the public esteem claimed by the Brahmins could only be obtained at the cost of deceitful attitudes: they were, indeed, systematically disqualified by the Jesuit, who underlined their propensity to lie and show themselves under false appearances.

Dubois also used the contractualists' vocabulary – *public esteem*, *public opinion*, *mutual consent* – in an inconsistent way. He pointed out that groups "which are despised in one district are often greatly *esteemed* in another". A few lines later, he admitted that the Shudra castes could be integrated into a hierarchy, a view confirmed by *public opinion*, "the surest guide of caste superiority" (1906: 23). He gave no example to support this assertion, simply declaring that "a very slight acquaintance with the customs of a province and with the private life of its inhabitants [would] suffice for fixing the position which each caste has acquired by *common consent* (*ibid.*: 48). However, he had just observed that, "[as] to the particular subdivisions [*jatis*] of each caste [*varnas*], it is difficult to decide the order of hierarchy observed amongst them"; a little further on, he even emphasized that it is not just difficult but downright "*impossible* to give precedence to any one [caste] in particular, the natives themselves not being agreed on that point" (*ibid.*, italics added). Hierarchy, a major stereotype of European thinking at the time, was being affirmed and denied simultaneously...

***

Murr converts Coeurdoux's apologetic intention into praise for caste hierarchy; the latter's unequivocal condemnation of Hinduism is transformed into an idyllic vision of the Brahmins, the caste system itself appearing as the ideal order to which France should return: "As the Brahmins embody the most perfect realization of this order", she writes, "[they] serve as a model to other Indians, and, through the author's discourse, to the French" (Murr 1987 b: 156-57, our translation).

India was the example of a perfect hierarchy. And Murr argues that by comparing Indian and French societies the Jesuit had arrived at a synthesis expressing the best of the two worlds: the excellence of European religion and the superiority of Indian society (*ibid.*: 165). She believes (or, rather, she imagines that Coeurdoux believed) that from such a synthesis a Utopia might emerge (*ibid.*). *Moeurs et coutumes des Indiens* was, from her perspective, a unique work, a manifestation of the open-mindedness of a Jesuit who had found in India the means to reflect upon himself and his own society.

Let us now return to Dubois whose text, according to Murr, had been "copied directly" from Coeurdoux's lost manuscript. It is impossible to know exactly the extent of the Abbé's plagiarism. But one thing is clear: Dubois *cannot* be read in the light of Murr's interpretation of *Moeurs et coutumes des Indiens*. The Abbé could not be more assertive in his condemnation of Indian civilization, which he considered hopelessly resistant to progress (1906: 96). The Hindus, he wrote, "will continue to grovel in poverty as long as their physical and intellectual faculties continue in the same groove" (*ibid.*). Such remarks were accompanied by eerie, gloomy thoughts: "To make a new race of the Hindus, one would have to begin by undermining the very foundations of their civilization, religion, and polity, and by turning them into atheists and barbarians" (*ibid.*). Dubois believed it was necessary to go back to a degree zero of history, the *tabula rasa* from which social life was supposed to have emerged. That was the prerequisite for European intervention:

> *Having accomplished this terrible upheaval, we might then perhaps offer ourselves to them as lawgivers and religious teachers. But even then our task would be only half accomplished. After dragging them out of the depths of barbarism, anarchy, and atheism into which we had plunged them, and after giving them new laws, a new polity, and a new religion, we should*

> *still have to give them new natures and different inclinations* (ibid.).

The end result of Dubois' reflections was certainly not the utopian ideal abstracted by Murr from Coeurdoux's work, but a programme of large-scale destruction of the traditional foundations of India and Hindu society.

CHAPTER-3

A QUEST FOR ORDER TAXONOMIC EXPERIENCES

I

Around 1806, James Mill conceived the ambitious project of writing a history of India. He essentially intended to draw a picture of the "great scene of British action", a work – more appropriately titled *The History of British India* – finally published in 1817. Even thus limited in scope, it involved enormous difficulties. Mill pointed out that to fully account for the transformations to be introduced by the British administration, it was necessary to evaluate the traditional institutions of India, her laws and form of government.

Mill emphasized the innovative character of his achievement: no writer before him had brought order to the state of dispersion and confusion of the available information. He had never been to India nor was he acquainted with any Indian language, but this was not seen as a drawback. Since a vast amount of data had already been collected and published in European languages, he believed "that a residence in India, or a knowledge of the languages of India, was (…) not indispensable" (*ibid.*: xiii). A full report could in no way be based on the testimony of a single man and, beyond certain limits, nothing justified direct observation. An individual would collect the facts to which he had immediate access; knowledge of languages would allow him to learn what had not been translated, obtaining through dialogue what books did not say. "This he can do", he admitted: "(but) I am not aware that he can do any thing further"; only the combined effort of several observers would provide "a competent knowledge of any extensive subject" (*ibid.*: xiv). In so far as relevant facts had already been recorded, someone "duly qualified may attain more knowledge of India, in one year, in his closet in England, than he could obtain during the course of the longest life, by the use of his eyes and his ears in India" (*ibid.*: xv).

In his opinion, no direct witness had the qualities required for the project he set out to accomplish. The servants of the East India Company were a case in point. They were "the foremost to declare, that their situation in India is such, as to preclude them from the acquisition of local knowledge" (*ibid.*: xx). This explained many of their errors: "We do not, we cannot, associate with the natives. We cannot see them in their houses, and with their families. (…) [W]e are, in fact, strangers in the land", Lord William Bentinck had written (*ibid.*: xxi). Sir Henry Strachey's comments were along the same lines:

> *We know little of their domestic life, their knowledge, conversation, amusements, their trades, and casts (...). The difficulty we experience in discerning truth and falsehood among the natives, may be ascribed, I think, chiefly, to our want of connexion and intercourse with them; to the peculiarity of their manners and habits; their excessive ignorance of our characters; and our almost equal ignorance of theirs* (ibid.: xxii).

Such assertions supported Mill's point of view: knowledge was not necessarily ensured by direct contact. Driven by a genuine search for truth, he opposed his own approach to that of the servants of the East India Company: "I have performed the business of research with a labour, and patience, which it would not be easy to surpass. And I believe there is no point, of great importance, involved in the History of India, which the evidence I have adduced is not sufficient to determine" (*ibid.*: xxiii).

Mill acknowledged the need for a wide range of testimonies, but he also claimed the right to choose the best of them. Like a judge faced with a multitude of evidence, the historian had to sort out the facts. He had to put together all the pieces of information that had been collected, compare them, weigh their relative plausibility and, finally, decide with discernment (*ibid.*: xviii-xix). The author irrevocably condemned the views of the Orientalists, those of William Jones in particular, even though he borrowed from them the bulk of the information he used. It was thanks to their translations of Sanskrit texts that he thought he had reconstituted crucial moments in India's ancient history.

After recalling the four orders (*varnas*), seen as "the first and simplest form of the division of labour and employments" (*ibid.*: 108), he alluded to the groups which, born from their inter-marriages, had ensured new professional specializations. "Having reached this stage", he wrote, "it does not appear that [Hindu society] has made, or that it is capable of making, much further progress" (*ibid.*: 120) – another way of saying that knowledge obtained through direct contact was "not indispensable"…

II

Mill's *History* has been evaluated from quite different points of view. It has been considered a "serious book" written by a "great English philosopher" (Kopf 1969: 236); "the first important history of India" (Thapar 1987 [1978]: 4); "the oldest hegemonic account of India within the Anglo-French imperial formation" (Inden 1990: 45); and the "most important source of British Indophobia and hostility to Orientalism" (Trautmann 1997: 117).

Eric Stokes had recognized in Mill's *History* "an attempt to make a philosophical analysis of Indian society and assess its place in the 'scale of civilization'" (1959: 53). In fact, this "place" had already been defined: India appeared to be the epitome of backwardness: "in beholding the Hindus of the present day we are beholding the Hindus of many ages past, and are carried back, as it were, into the deepest recesses of antiquity" (1817: 469). The essential features of their society were signs of "a people in the infancy of improvement". This point of view, the author believed, was confirmed by the philosophical conceptions of Jeremy Bentham. Pain and pleasure, the "two sovereign masters" of humanity, were said "to govern us in all we do, in all we say, in all we think" (1907 [1789]: 1). At the heart of Bentham's system was the idea of utility, the ability of all beings "to produce benefit, advantage, pleasure, good, or happiness". Utility was the means by which *every action whatsoever* should be approved or disapproved: "I say of every action whatsoever", Bentham wrote, "(…) not only of every action of a private individual, but of every measure of government" (*ibid.*: 2). The purpose of laws, and consequently of government, he believed, is to promote "the greatest happiness of the greatest number".

Pain and pleasure, misery and happiness were accepted by Mill as principles of a basic classification system that allowed the decisive moments of historical progress to be defined: "Exactly in proportion as *Utility* is the object of every pursuit, may we regard a nation as civilized". Conversely, "in proportion as its ingenuity is wasted on contemptible or mischievous objects (…) the nation may safely be denominated barbarous" (1817: 428).

These ideas were tirelessly reiterated regarding the form of government, justice, religion, customs, arts and science. Mill asserted that in every field, the attention of the Hindus had been focused on "frivolous observances" rather than on "objects of utility". But the theory was modified to justify the point of view previously adopted.

All the author sought to emphasize was the Indian way of thinking, which he deemed to be devoid of rigor and clarity. Indian legal conceptions were a perfect example: "It is not easy to conceive a more rude and defective attempt at the classification of laws (...), the most essential and obvious distinctions (being) neglected and confounded" (*ibid.:* 134). He concluded that "though no arrangement would appear more natural and more likely to strike even an uncultivated mind, than the division of laws, into civil and penal, we find the laws distinguished by these appellations, mixed and blended together in the code of the Hindus" (*ibid.*: 134-35).

These were also main features of Hindu religious ideas: "All is loose, vague, wavering, obscure, and inconsistent" (*ibid.*: 215). The highest expressions of religion were achieved when their goal was "the production of happiness"; but if "the sacred duties are made to consist in frivolous observances (...) we may be assured, the religious ideas of the people are barbarous" (*ibid.*: 263).

Exactly the same conclusions were abstracted from social rules of behaviour. The condition of women was particularly significant: "Among rude people, the women are generally degraded; among civilized people, they are exalted" (*ibid.*: 293). Only in a high state of civilization was attention given to the pleasures of life; and it was only in such circumstances "that the women, from their influence on those pleasures, begin to be an object of regard". This had not been the case in Hindu society: "A state of dependance more strict and humiliating than that which is ordained for the weaker sex among the Hindus cannot easily be conceived" (*ibid.*: 294).

Mill borrowed some of his information from Dubois whose ambiguous perspectives had been partially inspired, as we saw, by the contractualist theories about the origin of civil society. The arts and sciences had played a central role in that context: "I believe", the Abbé had written, "caste division to be in many respects the *chef-d'oeuvre*, the happiest effort, of Hindu legislation". In his words, the caste system allowed the development of arts and sciences, avoiding a return "into a state of barbarism" (1906: 28). Mill ignored this side of the argument. His perspective was again shaped by Bentham's conceptions. Acknowledging that the pleasures procured by the arts were a sign of progress, he asserted that the Hindus "little courted" them. Hindu artistic manifestations "are not merely void of attraction; they are unnatural, offensive, and not unfrequently disgusting" (*ibid.*: 354).

Science was a pretext for similar considerations. Astronomy and mathematics had developed in India for the sole "purposes of astrology, one of the most irrational of all imaginable pursuits; one of those which most infallibly denote a nation barbarous" (*ibid.*: 428).

The positive influcnce of the arts and sciences was therefore denied. Direct knowledge of India again proved unnecessary to sustain Mill's assertion that the caste system had made "but a few of the earliest steps in the progress of civilization" (*ibid.*: 429). The division into castes was a "degrading and pernicious system of subordination" – a system whose vices had been taken to the most "destructive height" (*ibid.*: 452). Like everything else, "the arts and sciences (…) [were] entirely correspondent" to the laws and institutions of the Hindus, a manifestation of "one of the rudest and weakest states of the human mind" (*ibid.*: 437).

III

Mill was appointed in 1819 to the executive government of East India House. This contributed to making his *History* recommended reading for the civil servants of the Company. For most of them, India was *British* India, described for a long time according to Mill's conceptions.

In the two extensive volumes of *A Geographical, Statistical and Historical Description of Hindostan and the Adjacent Countries*, published in 1820, Walter Hamilton presented to European readers a general outline of India – more precisely… of India since 1765. British supremacy had then been "so completely established" that native chiefs were relegated to "a very secondary importance". India was no longer to be seen as "a mere assemblage of Nabobs, Sultans, and Rajas". The country's political and economic landscape had been definitively altered by British laws and regulations.

The author started by declaring – as "a truth perfectly obvious" – that the interests of the British rulers "recommended the happiness of their native subjects" (1820, I: 93), a legacy of the Benthamite perspectives. In his essay titled *Government*, published in 1820, Mill himself had written that "power is a means to an end", and that this "end is every thing, without exception, which the human being calls pleasure" (in 1824: 9).

Hamilton added, nevertheless, that the government's main goal "was to discover what could be obtained from [the native subjects], not how they might be most benefited". Bentham's philosophy was tempered by the rulers' perspective: "In process of time (…), it became necessary to devise how ["native subjects"] might be benefited, in order that the same amount of resources might continue to be drawn from them" (Hamilton 1820, I: 93).

Regarding the relations between rulers and ruled, Hamilton insisted that the stability of the former depended on the ignorance and submission of the latter: "it is probable that since our effectual establishment in 1765, no native ever dreamed of subverting the government". Attention was drawn to the "completely despotic" nature of British authority in India, the submission of its subjects being "perfect and unqualified". Coercion or intimidation were therefore superfluous. "The sepoys", it was observed, "like the rest of the natives, are entirely uninstructed as to the form of government, policy of their rulers, or justice of their wars". It naturally followed that "our strength" rested on their "ignorance and apathy" (*ibid.*: 92).

The "place" of India in the scale of civilization had definitely been established. It was fully confirmed by the testimony of many authors – like Grant and Mill – that was often reproduced verbatim by Hamilton. The origin of his portrait of the Bengalis was easily recognizable: "to lie, steal, ravish, or murder, are not deemed crimes of sufficient atrocity to entitle the perpetrator to expulsion from society" (*ibid.*: 113). Such perspectives were not affected by the unexpected meanders of his sources:

> *After stating these heavy charges against the private character of the Bengalese, we must add, that as subjects they are quiet, patient, industrious, and governed with a facility almost incredible; and that one European may sleep secure, amidst a million of Bengalese, without a lock on his door, or a weapon of offence in his vicinity. We mention this as a notorious matter of fact, experienced by every European of character, who has ever resided among the genuine Bengalese, remote from the contamination of Calcutta, and of European society* (ibid).

Hamilton did not have precise information about castes. In his perspective, as in Mill's, they seemed to obey a hierarchical classification whose principles, however, he could not understand. He shared the equivocal point of view of most Europeans about Brahmins, noting their "undisputed" superiority but alluding to those who "degrade themselves by acting as spiritual instructors" to impure castes (*ibid.*: 109).

In his words, "the highest Sudras are the Vaidyas, or medical tribe", followed by the Kayasthas, or "writing caste". Following these, "are nine tribes of tradesmen [the Navasakhas] who, although greatly inferior to these scribes, are considered 'pure' Sudras" (*ibid.*) – as distinguished from those whose "origin is ascribed to the promiscuous intercourse" of the four *varnas* (*ibid.*: 110).

Here are the nine castes of tradesmen:

Druggists
Workers in shell
Coppersmiths
Cultivators of betel leaf
Weavers
Makers of garlands
Blacksmiths
Potters
Barbers

Table 3: *The Navasakhas* (ibid.: 109).

Hamilton did not explain why only the Navasakhas were chosen from among the huge diversity of Shudra castes. He could not grasp the logic organizing the whole: "by some strange caprice, not only the bankers, but also the goldsmiths are excluded from the pure castes of artificers, while barbers, pot makers, coppersmiths, and blacksmiths, obtain that much envied dignity" (*ibid.*: 109-110).

***

In *An Account, Geographical, Statistical, and Historical of Orissa Proper, or Cuttack*, Andrew Stirling considered it useful to sketch a global picture of the population. To this end, it seemed appropriate to refer to the comments produced in the 16th century by Abu'l Fazl, the famous minister of Akbar. He had "justly" portrayed the natives of Orissa as "very effeminate", "extremely deficient in manly spirit".

They were, in general, "ignorant and stupid" – features that made their cooperation in the service of the East India Company hardly advisable. Their blameworthiness was proverbial:

> *A striking proof of the estimation in which their capacity has been ever held, is the fact, that in all ages and under all governments since the downfall of the Orissan monarchy, the principal official employments throughout the province have been engrossed by foreigners (...), owing I really believe in a great measure to the difficulty of selecting from its indigenous population, persons properly qualified for trusts of difficulty and importance* (1825: 199).

Stirling was inspired by the commonplaces of the time. The people of Orissa were "well versed in all the arts of low cunning, dissimulation and subterfuge". Their manners were "sufficiently dissolute" – a consequence of "the obscene character, and impure symbols, of the demoralizing religions which they profess" (*ibid.*). But the author did his best to safeguard the pragmatic interests of the Company. From a set of more or less undifferentiated castes, he tried to identify the most helpful ones. A caste of Brahmin farmers – the Halia Brahmins (< Sanskrit *hala*, "a plough") – was one of them: "although not free from some of the vices of the Brahmin character, viz., audacity, stubbornness and mendacity, they are unquestionably the most enterprising, intelligent, and industrious of all the Company's *ryots* (…) in Orissa" (*ibid.:* 198-99).

The Company's purposes provided the beginning of structuring principles of organization. A simple dual "classification" made it possible to assimilate geographical discontinuities to degrees of intellectual development, psychological traits and forms of sociability: the "inhabitants of the hills, and of the jungles on the sea shore" were "shy", "sullen", "inhospitable", "uncivilized"; their chiefs were "grossly stupid, barbarous, debauched, tyrannical, and slaves of the most grovelling superstition" (*ibid.*: 200). The inhabitants of the plains, "whatever their faults", were quite different; they were "the most mild, quiet, inoffensive, and easily managed people, in the Company's provinces" – in other words, "a valuable class of servants" (*ibid.*: 199-200).

Stirling also alluded to the *varna* pattern of the Laws of Manu. Brahmins, Kshatriyas, Vaishyas and "pure" Shudras were mentioned – although "true" Kshatriyas seemed extinct in the region and Vaishyas were poorly represented there (*ibid.*: 195). But an attempt to introduce castes into the traditionally established divisions caused difficulties. Milkmen, Barbers, Husbandmen and others were *apparently* "genuine Súdras" (*ibid.*). Immediately below them were placed some of the "mixed groups", springing from intermarriage between *varnas*:

Gardeners
Iron smiths
Workers in shells
Weavers
Potters
Workers in bell metal
Carpenters
Painters
Goldsmiths

Fishermen
Physicians
Writers
Labourers
Candalas
(performing the lowest and most degrading offices)

Table 4: *"Mixed castes"* (ibid.: 196).

Like Hamilton, Stirling seemed to admit a vague order of precedence among the Shudras. But the lists produced by both authors showed sharp differences. Hamilton considered Potmakers and Blacksmiths to be "pure Shudras"; they were "impure", according to Stirling. Hamilton had placed the Navasakhas after Vaidyas and Kayasths. Stirling did otherwise. Physicians and Writers appear near the bottom of his list of "mixed castes" (Table 4), while some of the groups mentioned by Hamilton (Table 3) were placed (in a different sequence) at the top of his list.

Most European observers felt perplexed: "It is a chaos this multitude of castes", exclaimed Victor Jacquemont, who travelled in India between 1829 and 1832. "I suppose that those who claimed to find their way in this maze were no less lost than me" (1841: 282, our translation).

IV

"Caste", F. J. Shore wrote, "is a wide subject, difficult to be understood even by those who have mixed much among the people" (1837, II: 470). Like other authors before him, he pointed out that the current society appeared very different from the old *varnas* structure described in the Laws of Manu: Kshatriyas and

Vaishyas no longer existed "as separate classes". A vast number of groups (*jati*) had emerged (*ibid.*: 471-72) but their general features were hard to capture. An abundance of facts and regional diversities were obstacles to the apprehension of the global architecture. A huge variety of specificities – "an infinity of petty absurdities", in the author's perception – made it difficult to identify common denominators: "the contradictions and peculiarities of caste are so great in practice, that it is impossible to deduce any rule regarding it founded upon a general principle" (*ibid.*: 478).

George Campbell also departed from the Laws of Manu – a work that, far from alluding to a real society, attempted to define the social structure as "it *ought* to exist". The "infinite" variety of castes was understood by him as a system of a division of labour. The idea of a hierarchical arrangement crossed his mind but was finally dismissed:

> *There is doubtless a distinction of rank, some castes ranking higher than others; but, after all, it is most decidedly a division of labour or of clans, and not a division of rank. There is, in fact, no fixed general classification of the rank of castes – it is a mere matter of opinion, and exclusiveness is generally mutual. The higher castes have no considerable advantage over the lower in the material enjoyments of life, and when there is superiority it is rather political than the result of caste. A middle or inferior caste man retains his exclusiveness and his customs as much as one of high caste, and has not the least envy of the other, nor desire to change places* (1852: 67).

Benjamin Atkinson Irving admitted that Manu was a "dramatic personage, brought forward to give life and interest to a didactic composition, just as in the Republic, Plato introduces Socrates, Glaucon, Cephalus, and others, conversing together" in order to place "his opinions in a more attractive light than was possible in a set treatise" (1853: 15-6). Like Shore – from whom he borrowed much of his information – he stressed the incomprehensible character of Indian society.

The data gathered meanwhile by gazetteers and censuses needed to be properly organized; but the difficulty in grasping the essential features of the castes – a "mysterious subject" – made their classification problematic. The European ignorance of Indian reality was reflected in the structure of the censuses, which were based on vague or ill-adapted categories. In the *Census of the North West Provinces of the Bengal Presidency*, carried out in 1848, only a summary distinction between "agricultural" and "non-agricultural" communities had been drawn; and some key concepts – "house", "family" and others – had not been addressed with the desired precision (Christian 1854: 1-2).

Census operations raised enormous difficulties, even when implemented in geographically delimited areas. The working conditions in the field, the appointment of enumerators and the very nature of their relationship with respondents posed specific problems and also determined the results of the whole procedure. In 1866, the authors of the *Report on the Census of Calcutta* noted that the simplest written questionnaire could cause much confusion: "Considering the novelty of the undertaking, the suspicion that existed as to its scope and purposes, and the natural reluctance of the lower classes to afford information, it would have been unsafe to attempt too much" (1866: 5).

***

Authored by William Chichele Plowden in 1867. the report of the *Census of the North West Provinces* (1865) presented new classificatory perspectives. This was an adaptation to Indian realities of conceptions which had been introduced in the *Census of England and Wales for the year 1861*.

The extraordinary diversity of occupations brought about by the Industrial Revolution urgently required additional systematic organization. In this regard, a different method had been advocated by William Farr, an English physician and statistician. In 1841, he had joined the committee of the Statistical Society of London, which was responsible for providing technical advice on census operations. The importance of his intervention in this area having been widely recognized, the census of 1851 already included questions on physical disabilities. Later, he also drew attention to the need for a consistent classification of occupations and a solid foundation for the study of occupational disease (Eyler 1979). Classification had always aroused his interest, and it was in the old perspective of the natural sciences that he considered the organization of labour in England and Wales. In his opinion, the contemplation of nature inspired a perplexity analogous to that which resulted from the observation of the complex urban world in 19th century Europe:

> *Walk through a town. Who is now prepared to explain the distribution of houses, shops, manufactures, and trades – the number in each profession – the subordination of the men – the relations of the masters to each other – their connexion with the people of the country around (...)?* (Farr 1863: 225).

Employments had become "so numerous that the task of reducing them into scientific order appear(ed), at first sight, to be hopeless" (*ibid.*). Farr believed, however, that there is order beneath apparent chaos: "Universal order reigns in nature, and it is not likely to be absent from the regions of human industry. (…) It is certain that, amidst all confusions, order pervades the societies of men" (*ibid.*).

It seemed self-evident that "as man (…) has his place in the animal kingdom, so the working-men of various types form groups in the economic kingdom" (*ibid.*: 231). The author therefore proposed classifying occupations according to the hierarchical principles "adopted since the time of Linnaeus in the natural sciences".

The whole chain of nested groups generally used by taxonomists – varieties, species, genres, families, orders and classes – was not indispensable. Six Classes and eighteen Orders would be enough to define "men as producers":

Class	**Order**
(1) Professional	(1) Government of the Country (2) Defence of the Country (3) Learned Professions (Art, Literature, Sciences)
(2) Domestic	(4) Domestic Office or Duties of Wives, Mothers, Mistresses of Families… (5) Persons engaged in entertaining and performing Personal Offices for Man
(3) Commercial	(6) Persons who buy or sell, keep or lend Money, Houses, or Goods of various Kinds (7) Persons engaged in the Conveyance of Men, Animals, Goods, and Messages
(4) Agricultural	(8) Persons possessing or working the Land and engaged in growing Grains, Fruits, Grasses… (9) Persons engaged about Animals
(5) Industrial	(10) Persons engaged in Arts and Mechanic Productions (11) Persons working and dealing in the Textile Fabrics and in Dress (12) Persons working and dealing in Food and Drinks (13) Persons working and dealing in Animal Substances (14) Persons working and dealing in Vegetable Substances (15) Persons working and dealing in Minerals

(6) Indefinite and non Productive	(16) Labourers and other Branches of Labour undefined (17) Persons of Rank or Property not returned under any Office or Occupation (18) Persons supported by the Community, and of no specified Occupation

Table 5: *Hierarchical classification of occupations (according to William Farr).*

The belief in a natural order – denied by the naturalists themselves since the second half of the 18th century – was thus partially restored by Farr. It is true that when he presented his project, Louis Agassiz had already published *An Essay on Classification*, taking up the terms of an old debate:

> *The divisions of animals according to branch, class, order, family, genus, and species (...) seem to me to deserve the consideration of all thoughtful minds. Are these divisions artificial or natural? Are they the devices of the human mind to classify and arrange our knowledge (...) or have they been instituted by the Divine Intelligence as the categories of his mode of thinking?* (1859: 8).

Farr went further. Nothing was aleatory in the "marvelous economy of society" whose laws were homologous to those of the "phenomena of the heavens". The European division of labour was ultimately governed by the higher order of nature.

Oversimplified, Linnaeus' principles could also be adopted to classify the British-born subjects dwelling in India (as well as in other colonies and possessions). They were finally considered adequate for the Indian social reality as well and recommended by "two Committees of experts".

***

The transposition of Farr's model to the Indian universe naturally caused problems. In India, occupations as traditionally conceived, pass down from one generation to another and are inseparable from the caste system. A caste-specific occupation is an identity mark that unites all of the members of a group, including those who may never have performed such a task.

In the perspective of some Europeans, however, this should be "simplified". The caste institution, George Campbell had recently stated, was "nothing more than a great system of very minute hereditary division of labour" (1852: 68). *Nothing more*... The equivalence of caste and occupation was implied in this perspective. That was not, however, Plowden's view. Admitting that Indian means of livelihood could be subjected to the European statistical treatment, he postulated the arbitrary separation of occupation and caste. By uprooting the former – hereditary or not – from the latter, he fragmented a cohesive reality. "Occupations" *and* "castes" were, accordingly, independently addressed. Castes were relegated to an appendix of his report: a secondary – in fact, a totally meaningless – role was attributed to them. Mythical stories about their origin, loose references to the customs and habits of their members, among other subjects, were grouped, district by district, by supervisors' assistants whose comments testified to the lack of importance attached to their information: "I am not prepared to stake my official reputation on the accuracy of this record", wrote one of them (in Plowden 1867, Appendix B: 27). Another observed that "in the books which are available for reference the facts [about caste] are (...) so commingled with ridiculous traditions and ludicrous stories of mythology that it is very difficult to separate the one from the other" (*ibid*.: 49).

As for the means of livelihood themselves, the inadequacy of their distribution by Farr's Classes and Orders was promptly acknowledged. In some of Farr's categories "strange" occupations were introduced which, in any "civilized country", Plowden wrote, one would hesitate to mention: "There seems, however, to be no mock modesty among the 23 who described themselves as professional thieves, or among 321 pimps, 2,251 eunuchs, and 26,806 prostitutes". Many "curious characters" were also listed, including "professed mourners"; "alms-takers"; "pedigree-makers"; "men who describe themselves as 'flattering for gain'"; "ear-piercers"; "makers of caste-marks"; "wrestlers"; "charmers"; "fortune-tellers"; "jesters"; "mimics"; "hangmen"; "grave-diggers" (Plowden 1867: 87). What should one think of the "35 sturdy beggars" and the "974 bad characters" who have thus designated their modes of life? Plowden saw here "a display of whimsical humor" (*ibid.*: 86-7).

CHAPTER-4
NEW TAXONOMIC EXPERIENCES

I

The census of 1871/72 was planned as a statistical survey of the entire territory of British India. This project was not fully accomplished, but even in the form it was implemented, it was a herculean task. The vastness of the scrutinized regions, the short time available for the work, the scant knowledge of local specificities and insufficient staff preparation accounted for the imperfection of the undertaking.

Each census operation implied a multiplicity of tasks to be performed by different officers: enumerators, assistant supervisors, local clerks, district officers and provincial superintendents. Step by step, the information moved further and further away from the area where it had been collected, and it sometimes appeared hazardous to reach definitive conclusions. As William W. Hunter, the Director-General of Statistics to the Government of India, was forced to recognize, "it would be unwise for a central compiler, drawing his materials from so distant and widely-separated sources, to hope (...) he had obtained a complete success" (1875: x).

Many factors accounted for the often-admitted short comings of the final results, the first of them frequently being attributed to the Indian field officers. According to H. Beverley, the Inspector-General of Registration in Bengal, "ignorance, indolence, stupidity, and dishonesty were at all times active sources of error, against the evil consequences of which the superintendents had ever to be on the guard" (1872: 74). C. F. Magrath, Inspector of Registration offices who had been in charge of the Patna branch, expressed himself in identical terms: "no little confusion arose from the utter carelessness of the Kayesths, who formed the major portion of the enumerators" in Bihar (Magrath 1872: 156). Allegedly devoid of critical capacity, they were charged with passively recording whatever information they received, no matter how absurd it might seem from a European perspective.

Although it became increasingly evident that the forms included badly worded questions or questions ill-suited to the context, the condemnation of the enumerators was recurrent. The enumerators were, however, the *sine qua non* of the whole operation. More than elsewhere, they played a very unique role here. Usually selected from among the inhabitants of the areas under scrutiny, they helped to overcome the proverbial resistance to door-to-door inquiries. They were generally unpaid: the official status they were invested with was supposed to be a sufficient reward and sometimes they were even expected to pay for their travel expenses. Many of them, as they walked through the maze of the creeks and rivers of the Bay of Bengal, "incurred expenses for boat-hire, which (...) could not always be reimbursed" (Beverley 1872: 26). Those who had to trek through jungles, often found themselves in extremely adverse conditions, which sometimes put their lives at risk.

Their profile varied from region to region. Teachers and students were recruited wherever a school existed. Village headmen, landlords, agriculturists, merchants and shopkeepers were also candidates for the task – insofar as they knew how to read and write. But in certain districts the enumerators were nearly as uneducated as the often-illiterate householders. In a number of instances, they were only able to write their name and needed assistance to prepare the final returns.

In Orissa, leaves from date-palm trees were traditionally used to write and draw on with an iron style: "The most facile writers on palm leaves, however, are but sorry caligraphists with pen and ink; and it became a question therefore how the printed forms were to be filled up by the great bulk of the enumerators" (*ibid.*: 36). More time and human resources were required. According to the then Collector of Cuttack,

> *Considerable difficulty was anticipated, and indeed experienced in many parts of the district, in obtaining competent men as enumerators, and it would have been impossible to have taken a simultaneous census by means of the printed forms, as persons who could write on paper were not obtainable. The difficulty was got over by allowing the census to be taken in such places on palm-leaves, the entries being subsequently copied by the supervisors, the police and other Government servants, in printed forms* (ibid.: 38).

In the words of W. R. Cornish, the Sanitary Commissioner for Madras, the work of the enumerators "was done in a perfunctory manner"; better results would perhaps be obtained in the future if small remunerations were granted "to those village officials, whose figures stand the test of a rigid scrutiny" (1874: 31). But what could such a test be?

***

Jat, *jati*, the Indian terms translated as "caste", may refer to different contexts and this aroused the perplexity of Westerners. What in fact was a caste? It seemed incomprehensible that such a *simple* question remained unanswered. But, in this regard, the purported incompetence of the enumerators reflected a "general ignorance". If every Hindu knew little about the group into which he was born, his lack of concern for his neighbours was still greater. "Whatever a native may know of the customs of his own peculiar branch, he is, as a rule, grossly ignorant of the habits and customs, or the origin, of those outside the pale of his own section of the community"; this was "a subject upon which no two divisions, or sub-divisions, of the people themselves are agreed" (*ibid.*: 116). The very word "caste" often seemed to be used in an inappropriate way: among the lower groups, "there is a great tendency to substitute a title for their caste, by way of being taken for something better than they are" (Magrath 156).

The distinction between "high" and "low" castes was also open for discussion:

> *The French Government of Pondicherry, and our own British Government, have frequently been asked to define what is a "high" caste and what a "low" caste, but our administrators, not at all ambitious of pulling the proverbial hornet's nest about their ears, have prudently declined to attempt a definition of this knotty point* (Cornish 1874: 130).

In Cornish's perspective, the divergences on this subject led to the questioning of the idea of a global Hindu social structure. The relation between "Twice-Born" and Shudras was analogous, according to him, to that which had prevailed in England between Normans and Saxons. Among the three higher *varnas* "there are no contentions as to place and position, but it is not so with the great mass of aboriginal inhabitants, who accepted the position of Súdras under the caste system of the Aryans. Here every sub-division contends for a better position than the one it occupies in public esteem". The opposition between "high" and "low" castes was seen as the result of a historical process: "Some of the so called 'low' castes, and Pariahs, represent a people who were supreme in Southern India" before the introduction of the caste system; as for "purity of descent", claimed by the higher *varnas*, it seemed "sometimes more than dubious". Castes would be no more than the residue of a remote past: "any attempt to define the respective positions of each caste would only help to perpetuate a social peculiarity, which has lived its day" (*ibid.*).

***

In his assessment of the census reports of 1871/72, Henry Waterfield recognized the unsatisfactory results regarding "caste". This was due, in his words, "partly to the intrinsic difficulties of the subject, and partly to the absence of a uniform plan of classification" (1875: 20). These two reasons were actually one and the same. "Caste" had resisted any attempt at systematic reflection and, *therefore*, any consistent plan of classification. But the embarrassment regarding the "classification of caste" was just part of something larger and more delicate: classification *tout court*. To begin with, was it possible to approach the subject of castes without simultaneously addressing that of tribes? Close relationships between them had been established in several contexts, some tribes being no longer exempt from the influence of castes.

W. W. Hunter had dismissed the *varna* theory of Manu, which presented, according to him, "a stiffness and an inertia (...) very discouraging to Indian social reformers" (1868: 100). Taking up a perspective that had been generalized by Max Müller, he argued that the ethnic composition of Bengal could be reduced to just two elements: "Aryan invaders" and "Aboriginals" (*ibid.*: 111). In Beverley's words, this was too simplistic a view: in no other part of India did one find such ethnic diversity; much more had to be done "before any correct classification of the people of Bengal according to their ethnical affinities [could] be finally laid down" (Beverley 1872: 153). In his own attempt, he had still been guided "by the stereotyped, though somehow exploded, four-fold classification of Manu" (*ibid.*: 154). But his views partially rested on those proposed by Magrath – who did not accept Manu's conceptions. Magrath also rejected Hunter's opposition between Aryans and non-Aryans, arguing that an intermediate class of semi-Hinduized aborigines should be recognized: "Like the colours in the rainbow, the jungle tribes draw steadily nearer and nearer to the Hindus, and the Hindus of lower caste as steadily mingle with the Hinduised jungle tribes" (Magrath 1872: 160). Beverley did not accept that either: the idea of insensitive gradations was of no help to him, even if he was ready to reconsider many hastily established categories.

A religious classification of groups had been prescribed by the Government of India: "*Hindus*", "*Muhammadans*", "*Christians*", "*Buddhists*" and "*Others*". However, in the official forms, the term "Hindus" was used in a double sense, racial and religious. The first meaning implied an Indian origin: "All natives of India were broadly spoken of as Hindus"; in the second, the term referred to all those who were not Muslims. The aboriginal tribes were thus supposed to be put under the "Others" heading. This caused new difficulties. Beverley had been "reminded by high authority that Hindus are only heathen, little differing from the aboriginal tribes" (Beverley 1872: 129). What did that "little difference" consist of? Where could one draw the boundary line between "Hindus" and "Others"? Since some tribal societies were partially Hinduized, how could one distinguish "pure Hindus" from low-caste people practicing some form of Hinduism? What would "the test of faith [be] which is to distinguish the real Hindu from the semi-Hinduized aboriginal?" (*ibid.*).

Beverley struggled with commonsensical definitions such as "pure" Hindus and "semi-Hinduized aboriginals". But unlike Magrath, he demanded exact lines of demarcation. He was looking for the *right* definition of Hinduism, even if he knew that "no one has ventured as yet to lay down any such definition" (*ibid.*). Doubts remained. As observed by C. Bernard, officiating secretary to the Government of Bengal, Beverley showed "the difficulty of settling *who are and who are not Hindoos*, and has mentioned that the people put under 'Hindoos', when classified by religions, comprise many *who are not* Hindoo by race, and *scarcely so in any other sense*" (in Beverley, 1872: 3, italics added).

Referring to the work of Edward Tuite Dalte, Beverley ended up considering "Aboriginal tribes" and "Semi-Hinduized Tribes" (distributed by geographical areas) in addition to castes that were organized according to their traditional occupations. Large sets were then proposed: Brahmins and Rajputs; Agricultural castes; Weaving castes; Labouring castes, etc.. Within each set, particular castes were generally presented alphabetically.

The authors of the various reports had taken "great pains (...) in the classification of the population according to caste"; in the absence of a common system, each writer had adopted "that which seemed to him best suited for the purpose" (Waterfield 1875: 20). We saw, however, that the adoption of Farr's classificatory criteria led to the devaluation of castes. The topic was now approached from a historical point of view, in an independent section of the report authored by F. S. Growse – *Caste: its Origin and Development.*[1]

II

The attempt to adapt Farr's classificatory model to Indian reality, with the consequent split between "castes" and "occupations", imposed a new and unexpected outlook on the Hindu social system. The idea of a radical rupture was not always

1. Published thereafter, without major modifications, as an Appendix to *Mathurá. A District Memoir* (Growse 1882).

accepted, but any effort to rebuild the lost unity inevitably perpetuated the memory of separation. In this respect, the Madras census for 1871 must be singled out. C. E. Gover, an official of the Madras' Municipality and former Secretary to the Madras Town Census Committee (1869), had started to write the relevant report. He died in 1872 and Cornish was requested to take up the unfinished work. The credit for the results obtained, Cornish wrote, should be granted "mainly to Mr. Gover's foresight" (1874: vii), although it is not easy to identify exactly the part played by each author.

Chapter XII, *The Occupations of the People*, had been "arranged on the principles laid down in the Madras Town Census Report" and corresponded "in most important particulars with the system of classification proposed by Dr. Farr" (*ibid.*: 176). Nineteen sub-divisions (instead of the original eighteen headings) were now considered, along with some other modifications:

Main groups	Sub-divisions
I : Professional	1. Government Service, Civil 2. Military and Police 3. Learned Professions 4. Minor Professions
II : Domestic	5. Personal Service
III : Commercial	6. Traders 7. Conveyers
IV : Agricultural	8. Cultivators
V : Industrial	9. Dress and textile fabrics 10. Food, drink, and stimulants 11. Metals 12. Construction 13. Books 14. Household goods 15. Combustibles

VI : Indefinite and Non-productive	16. Laborers for hire 17. Property 18. Unproductive 19. Others

Table 6: *Classification of occupations according to Gover* (Cornish 1874: 176).

But Cornish – and Gover? – considered it possible to use Farr's classification of *occupations* in order to describe the transformations undergone by certain *castes* under British influence. This was, of course, a totally new perspective which inevitably affected the very structure of the report.

The Chapter entitled *The Occupation of the People* was preceded by the Chapter *Castes* – where Farr's classificatory model was first introduced, albeit in a surreptitious manner. Let us consider the decisive passage:

> *[The Committee of the Madras Town Census] started with the assumption that the present Hindu castes must all have branched out from a few parent stems; that from the first there must have been a primitive division of labor, and hence of caste, corresponding to the great division of labor now existing,* i.e., Professional, Personal service, Commercial, Agricultural, Industrial, and Non-Productive (*ibid.: 116-17*).

This is one of the oddest episodes in the history of censuses in British India. Although Farr's name *is not mentioned here*, the six main categories of his model merge into a kind of "etiological myth" – a story about the origin of the "mixed classes", obviously inspired by the Sanskrit tradition. The theory of Manu, which underlies this passage, is also reflected in the social classification proposed by the Committee. The "twice-born" – (1) the Priesthood (Brahmins), (2) the Warrior Castes (Kshatriyas) and (3) the

Trading Castes" (Vaishyas) – were followed by Shudra castes, plus "Out-castes" and "Aboriginals":

1. Agricultural or cultivating Castes.
2. Shepherd and Pastoral Castes.
3. Artisan Castes.
4. Writer or Accountant Castes.
5. Weaver Castes.
6. Agricultural and Servile Castes … (chiefly employed as laborers or slaves of Class 1).
7. Pot-making Castes.
8. Mixed classes (chiefly of religious sects renouncing caste distinctions, and connected with temple service and worship).
9. Fishing and Hunting Castes.
10. Palm-cultivating Castes.
11. Barber Castes.
12. Washerman Castes.
13. Lower races, now regarded as out-castes or Pariahs, but in some of their divisions, the representatives of the aborigines of India.

Table 7: *Shudra groups, Out-castes, Aborigines* (ibid.:117).

The sets in the Table above do not fit any specific order: they were randomly assembled with the sole purpose of ascertaining that "nearly the whole population could be conveniently grouped under one or the other heading" (*ibid.*). Nor were they related to the "great divisions of labor now existing" – which had initially been mentioned.

***

It is difficult to believe that Cornish could have taken these conjectures seriously. He did not hide his scepticism about his contemporaries' ideas on the caste system: no research on the subject had succeeded in reducing "into order and classification the almost innumerable sub-divisions which still go on extending amongst the people" (*ibid.*: 116). Cornish was particularly critical of the classical theory on the origin of the *varnas* and the "mixed classes".[2] However, this was precisely the perspective he himself presented at the beginning of his Chapter on "castes". The fact seems to prove his indulgence towards the conceptions of the Committee of the Madras Town Census, which were in line with Gover's views. Such an approach was not free from imperfection but it represented, Cornish admitted, an "attempt at simplifying the abstruseness which now surrounds the whole question" (*ibid.*).

A new allusion to the "great divisions of labor" reappears in the last part of the Chapter on castes. We find here, for the first time in full (six main groups and nineteen sub-divisions) the diagram which will not be explicitly attributed to Farr until the following Chapter.

Cornish's goal – or was it still Gover's? – was to draw attention to a particular aspect of the recent history of certain castes. The returns regarding "occupations" had showed how far the male Brahmin population "have kept to the legitimate employments of their caste, and in what way they have departed from the rule of life which the *Shástras* lay down for them" (*ibid.*: 133).

Roughly 60 percent of that population was distributed as follows:

2. W. W. Hunter and J. W. Nelson were, in Cornish's words, "the only authors I have met with who take a philosophical view of the subject of caste. Dr. Hunter (…) has shown very clearly that the Brahmans of the present day are not of uniform origin, and Mr. Nelson (…) has explained that the caste system of Menu never had vitality in Southern India" (*ibid.*: 116, note).

	No. employed	Percentage
(I) Professional:		
Government Civil Service	8,837	1.6
Military or Police Service	747	0.1
Learned Professions	18,499	3.4
Minor Professions	55,504	10.2
(II) Domestic:		
Personal Service	19,584	3.6
(III) Commercial:		
Traders	12,910	2.4
Conveyers	969	0.2
(IV) Agricultural:		
Cultivators	132,443	24.2
(V) Industrial:		
Dress	165	0.03
Food	1,778	0.3
Metals	20	0.003
Construction	55	0.01
Books	40	0.007
Household goods	16	0.003
Combustibles	11	0.002
(VI) Indefinite and Unproductive:		
Laborers	5,384	1.0
Property	64,545	11.7
Unproductive	15,529	2.9
Others	1,898	0.3

Table 8: *Brahmin castes according to occupations* (ibid.: 133-34).

Some Brahmins had been admitted into the military and police departments of the government (first and second sub-divisions of Group I); in the third and fourth sub-divisions ("Learned and minor professions") of the same Group were placed lawyers, doctors, family and temple priests, astrologers, almanack makers... Traders and conveyers (Group III) could also be found. But the most "extraordinary revelation" concerned the high percentage of those involved in agriculture: they had become landlords. Cornish saw here the expression of the worldly ambitions of this group of people: they had "gradually shifted their position from that of mere priests, teachers, and beggars, to the more substantial one of a landed aristocracy" (*ibid.*: 135).

In other words, castes were now perceived in the light of the Western system of occupations. Brahmins subsisting on alms – leading "a mendicant life, according to the primary rules of their order" (*ibid.*: 136) – were now a minority, since relying "on the bounty of the charitable" was no longer meritorious; "more honorable" means of livelihood could be chosen. Those who still had such an existence were placed "amongst the unproductive class" – that is, equated with European vagrants...

III

Plowden was appointed General Commissioner for the Census of 1881. He still felt unable to deal with castes, considered an "intricate" and "complex" topic; this time, he began nevertheless by attempting to arrange them according to social position. The project was quickly discarded:

> *Petitions were sent in to my office and to the offices of the Deputy Superintendents of Census in the Provinces complaining of the position assigned to castes to which the petitioners belonged; and the whole subject was shrouded in so much uncertainty and*

> *obscurity that the original arrangement was dropped* (1883: 277).

Plowden now admitted that Farr's classification system was not suited to "a country where the conditions of life and the circumstances of the people differ materially from those prevailing in Western Europe" (*ibid.*: 347). But no other system seemed to be more advantageous. Farr's model was thus kept, this time with Classes, Orders and Sub-Orders.

As before, certain "occupations" – those of private trackers, jokers and story-tellers, earpickers, pigeon-flyers, makers of lime preparation for killing hairs, pimps, panders, prayer-mutterers, curers by incantation, etc. – aroused perplexity. They still had a "strange sound to English ears" and could perhaps be considered superfluous. Given, however, "the small amount of knowledge we really possess as to the trades and crafts of the population of our provinces it is better to err on the side of collecting too much than too little" (*ibid.*). Castes continued to be relegated to a secondary plan.

J. A. Bourdillon, author of the *Report on the Census of Bengal, 1881*, also acknowledged the failure of the transposition of the European classification system. Even if one could admit the accuracy of the data collected by the enumerators, "the statistical value of the tables in which they are shown would not have been very great, because the system of classification which has been adopted is not altogether suitable for India" (*ibid.:* 168).

The most important professions in England either had no real counterpart or were weakly represented in Bengal. Moreover, a literal translation of English concepts proved to be misleading in many cases: "the farmer in England is a very different person from the man who bears the same name in Bengal" (*ibid.*: 170). Unfortunately, it was "too late to reopen the whole question of classification" (*ibid.*: 168).

In his *Report on the Census of the Panjab of 1881*, Denzil Ibbetson continued to adopt the distinction between "caste" and "occupation" while emphasizing the ineffectiveness of the method persistently recommended. A rigorous classification proved impossible. But some form of classification was imperative, even if the results were acknowledged to be poor. Consider the following distribution of the population:

1. Landowning and agricultural tribes and castes;
2. Religious, Professional, Mercantile, and Miscellaneous Castes;
3. Vagrant and criminal tribes, gypsies, menials and artisans.

The second of these groups included "some of the highest and some of the lowest castes in the Province" (1916 [1883]: 214). The criterion chosen for assembling them is surprising: the castes in question, we are told, are "all those that are left after separating the landowning and agricultural castes on the one hand, and the vagrant, artisan, and menial classes on the other" (*ibid.*).

An operation of this kind could only lead to an "exceedingly heterogeneous collection" – an indefinable set: "as a whole" it occupied "a position superior to that of the landowning classes if measured by a religious standard", but was "indefinitely inferior if the comparison be made from a social or political standpoint" (*ibid.*: 27).

These are the broad groups that were presented:

1. Priestly Classes
2. Ascetic and Mendicant Orders
3. Minor Professional Castes
4. Mercantile and Shop-Keeping Castes
5. Carrier and Peddler Castes
6. Miscellaneous Castes

The third of the above categories – "Minor Professional Castes" – gave rise to new perplexities: "I have felt great doubt as to how I should class and where I should place the castes which I have included in this group" (*ibid.*: 230). Some of them, although of a very low status, "are in some measure allied to the priestly classes" because they are "invested with a sort of *quasi*-sacred character" (*ibid.*). That was the case for the Nai, the Barber, whose occupation was "considered degrading". As part of his duties, he "shaves and shampooes the villagers, prepares tobacco for the village rest-house, and attends upon the village guests" (*ibid.*). But he "is much more than a barber". He is "the hereditary bearer of formal messages from one village to another, such as news of auspicious events, formal congratulations, letters fixing the date of weddings, and the like" (*ibid.*). The semi-priestly Nai and the Brahmin formed "the embassy sent to conclude a betrothal"; and, in the context of wedding ceremonies, the Nai played "an important part, next indeed to that of the Bráhman himself" (*ibid.*). Let us pause here.

In Ibbetson's words, the "Priestly Classes" included groups who were "by no means purely priestly": some of them were "large owners and cultivators of land" (*ibid.*: 215). It follows that not all large landowners were placed under the same heading; and that Brahmins did not have to be priests to be members of the "Priestly Classes". The situation of the Nái was quite different. Although he was invested with a *quasi-sacred* character and was endowed with *semi-priestly* functions, he could only be classified under "Minor Professional Castes". In other words, a Brahmin who was less than a priest was still a priest; but a Nai, even if considered "much more that a barber" was still, after all, a barber and nothing but a barber…

Doubts and difficulties made the following question inevitable: "Why (…) was the English system of classification adopted?" Only one answer was possible: "We had no other"…

CHAPTER-5

"A MIGHTY MAZE WITHOUT A PLAN..."

I

By the end of the 19th century, misunderstandings about caste persisted "not for lack of matter", Eustace John Kitts wrote, "but from its abundance and complexity, and a lack of all rational arrangement". "The subject as a whole has indeed been a mighty maze without a plan" (1885: v).

Having accepted Farr's Classes and Orders as appropriate categories for labour statistics, Plowden arbitrarily detached the castes from their "hereditary or customary" occupations. Kitts tried to reunite what Plowden had separated but he simply introduced castes into Farr's model. Classes and Orders were preserved along their broad lines, Orders being sub-divided into Groups and Groups encompassing castes and tribes arranged by linguistic families. "Hereditary" occupations were thus subordinated to the logic of the "official" means of livelihood (*ibid.*: 49-55). Castes, alphabetically indexed within each Group, continued to form anarchic sets that were totally disconnected from their ethnographic context.

The year Kitts published his work, John Collinson Nesfield proposed a conjectural reconstruction of the history of Indian civilization, highlighting major stages of human progress. "Function, and function only", in his opinion, "was the foundation upon which the whole caste system of India was built up" (1885: 88). The supposed overall hierarchy of castes would preserve the memory of a historical evolution, a process that could explain the "social importance and respectability" of each group and the particular activity assigned to it. Refusing the division between Aryans and Aboriginals, the author assumed "the unity of the Indian race".

In 1885, twelve years after his arrival in India as a colonial administrator, Herbert Hope Risley was commissioned to conduct an ethnographic survey of Bengal. This was the beginning of a search that also led – by other means – to the idea of social hierarchy:

> *[We] may perhaps venture to compare the social gradations of the Indian caste system to a series of geological deposits. The successive strata in each series occupy a definite position determined by the manner of their formation, and the varying customs in the one may be said to represent the fossils in the other. The lowest castes preserve the most primitive customs, just as the oldest geological formations contain the simplest form of organic life* (1891 b, I: xxvii-xxviii).

Risley abandoned the criterion of professional specialization, though: race, according to him, was the origin of the caste system.

***

Census operations had provided a great amount of information on different aspects of Indian social reality. But "in reading any standard English work on ethnology", Risley noted, "there is nothing that an Indian official is more inclined to regret than the comparatively scanty use that has been made of the great storehouse of ethnological facts which English rule in India has opened to inquirers in Europe" (1886: 71). He was determined to change this state of things.

Favourable conditions existed in India for conducting large-scale ethnographic surveys and in-depth ethnological studies, but it was necessary to reconsider the data through adequate scientific perspectives. In 1885, Paul Topinard had published *Eléments d'Anthropologie Générale*, a book that offered Risley a point of view he considered suitable. This work, with comparative anatomy as its central pillar, aimed at a classification of human groups through physical characteristics (colour of the skin; hair; nasal or cephalic index). The method proved largely redundant: it attempted to provide "scientific" confirmation of what could be seen by the naked eye. Analysis legitimized fundamental types "created by a kind of provisional synthesis" and intuitively recognized by "all travelers and anthropologists" (Topinard 1885: 288, our translation). This point of view was promptly adopted:

> *The scientific methods which anthropometry prescribes attempt to fix vague personal impressions by reducing them to statistical formulas. No one could mistake a Brahman for a Kol, but the most minute verbal description of their characteristic differences of feature falls far short of the numerical analysis that can be arrived at by measuring specific dimensions of the head, nose, cheekbones, orbits, forehead, and zygomatic arches* (Risley 1891 b, I: xxx).

Risley believed that anthropological measurements would help to clarify "the origin of the component elements of the population of Bengal" (1886: 74). But he acknowledged the tentative nature of the approach: "In dealing with the castes and customs of forty-five millions of people, some working hypotheses are essential if one is not to wander blindly in a maze of conflicting facts" (*ibid.*: 75).

Alfred Lyall had recently stressed that the gradual absorption of non-Aryan populations via the caste system determined a partial transformation of their way of life, including the adoption of a new language and different religious conceptions (1882, chapter V). Risley admitted he could describe the social stratification supposedly inherent in this process but the ranks of his conjectural hierarchy were represented not by discrete tribal communities, but by heterogeneous sets of tribes whose status were allegedly defined by Hindu *public opinion*. Nothing is convincing in the general argument of this text, which also seems to be dominated by a teleological intention. We will come back to this soon.[1]

***

From Risley's anthropometric perspective, miscegenation was a setback. The ancient populations of Europe, to take just one example, had merged and their original physical characteristics had faded away. The process of *métissage* "tends to complicate the investigations and to obscure and confuse the results". In this regard, the subcontinent was seen as an exceptional laboratory: "In India, whatever may have been the case centuries ago" (1891 a: 239), crossbreeding was no longer possible.

Whatever may have been the case ... Risley arbitrarily isolated a specific time period. Overlooking what might have happened *before* the integration of the tribal communities into the caste system, the author only considered the period during which miscegenation had been discouraged. From a certain point in time, he believed, everything had changed: caste imposed the distribution

1. As C. J. Fuller has noted, a continuing disagreement in this regard "actually pointed to the common absence of any consensus about the order of social precedence, so that Risley was searching for certainty where it did not exist" (2024: 133).

of the population into "mutually exclusive aggregates of homogeneous composition". Intermarriages were prohibited, so "differentiation rather than integration" was the inevitable consequence, the fact by virtue of which each group had preserved its essential physical features.

Taking into account the ratio of nasal breadth to nasal length – to which Topinard had accorded a high degree of accuracy – Risley opposed Dravidians and Aryans, "two widely distinct types, the one platyrhine to a degree closely approaching to the negro, and the other leptorhine in much the same measure as the population of Southern Europe" (*ibid.*: 252). He believed that a whole gradation could be found between the two types; that was the result of "the intermixture of members of the extreme types and their descendants" (*ibid.*). Intermarriages had therefore taken place not only *before* but also *after* the integration of tribal populations into the caste system. It followed that the strict nature of the rules of endogamy had to be reviewed: "the rigid enforcement of the caste principle at the present day renders (…) intermixture impossible, but it may be gathered from the account of the caste system given in the so-called Institutes of Manu that the rule of endogamy was less stringent in earlier times" (*ibid.*).

Despite the fragilities of his argument, Risley did not hesitate to present a general formula as if it had been abstracted from a laboratory experiment:

> *Take the fifteen castes of Bengal Proper, the two castes of Behar, the seventeen castes of Chota Nagpore, and the twenty-three castes of the North-West Provinces for which [the] index has been measured, arrange them in the order of the nasal index, putting the lowest or most leptorhine index at the top, and it will be found that the order thus arrived at corresponds substantially with the order of social precedence* (ibid.: 253).

A provisional conclusion was then put forward: "Within certain geographical boundaries it may be laid down at least as a working hypothesis, if not as an absolute law, that the social position of a caste varies inversely as its nasal index" (*ibid.*). This strange statement suggested that the anthropometric measurements should be ordered *sequentially*. The two racial types – leptorhine and platyrhine – defined the summit and the basis of a gradation of nasal indices. Of course, the linear order thus arbitrarily forged had an undeclared purpose. Meaningless in themselves, anthropometric measurements could only acquire relevance in *correspondence* with something else: "The most notable feature of [the] statistics of the nasal index", Risley wrote, "is (...) their correspondence with – I should perhaps say their concomitant variation in relation to – two other sets of facts independently ascertained" (*ibid.*: 252).

The two sets of facts in question – social precedence and specific conceptions of exogamy – had been the subject of *Primitive Marriage in Bengal* (1886); they became the main support for the 1891 hypothesis. Specific sociological features had then been presented as characteristic of opposed status in a "hierarchical" arrangement, supposedly recognized by Hindu public opinion: "At the bottom of the social system, as understood by the average Hindu, stands a large body of non-Aryan tribes and castes". They were divided into exogamous sections, each claiming to be descended from an ancestor whose spirit took the form of a plant or animal (*ibid.*: 75). Such totemic conceptions were considered characteristic of the most primitive state of civilization. At the other end of the evolutionary scale, representing "the top of Hindu society" (*ibid.*: 81), were placed

> *the Brahmans, and the large body of castes which ape Brahmanical customs, divided into exogamous sections* (gotras), *the members of which profess to be descended from the mythical* rishi *or inspired saint whose name*

> *the* gotra *bears. (...) Exogamous sections of this kind may conveniently be styled* eponymous (*ibid.*: 82).

Eponymic exogamous sections and *totemic exogamous sections* typified the "top" and "bottom" of the hierarchical structure drawn up by Risley. This order of social precedence, he stated in 1891, matched his sequence of anthropometric measurements.

The question of social precedence in India had never been seriously debated, but Risley believed that *Primitive Marriage in Bengal* provided the data that confirmed the plausibility of his thesis: social hierarchy was the backbone of his statistics of the nasal index. Let us take a closer look at this hierarchical structure.

"Top" and "bottom" were intended to circumscribe an uncharted "intermediate zone" about which Risley could say nothing. But the extremes themselves were imprecise sets of undefined elements. We have just noted that, at "the top" of the social structure, were not only Brahmins – the prototype of the groups with eponymic exogamous sections (*gotras*) – but all the castes who had adopted their model. To be precise, no true *gotras* exist among castes belonging to Kshatriya or Vaishya *varnas*: "By a sort of authorized fiction, however, these castes were permitted to adopt the *gotras* of the family priests of their ancestors, and this practice has now spread by imitation to other castes in Bengal" (*ibid.*: 82) – to Vaidyas, Kayasths and many other Shudra groups (*ibid.*: 82-3). Strangely enough, the model of castes with eponymous exogamous sections – the distinctive feature of those placed at the "top" – included groups belonging to *all varnas*...

Now let us turn to the "bottom". It comprised "the large body of non-Aryan tribes and castes" that had exogamous sections bearing "the name of an animal, a tree, a plant, or of some material object, natural or artificial, which the members of that [section] are prohibited from killing, eating, cutting, burning, carrying, using, etc." (*ibid.*: 75). Who had selected the criteria allowing the inclusion of all these groups in the same series? Who had proclaimed their unity and placed them *en bloc* at the bottom of the structure? Did the procedures adopted express the point of view of the "average Hindu"? In fact, only relatively extended ethnographic knowledge would have made it possible to achieve such a generalization.

Consider how the "non-Aryan tribes and castes" were hierarchically classified. The "lower" level would be occupied by different groups such as those found "among the Kolarian Sonthals [Santals] and the Dravidian Oraons, both of whom still retain their original language, worship non-Aryan gods, and have a fairly compact tribal organization" (*ibid.*: 75-6). The Bhumijs of Western Bengal and Orissa illustrated a "step higher in the social scale, according to Hindu estimation" (*ibid.*: 76). They had generally lost their original language and now spoke Bengali. They worshiped Hindu gods as well as tribal "fetishistic deities". Some of their leaders had secured the collaboration of "a low class of Brahmans" (*ibid.*: 77). Above the Bhumijs, "at a further stage in the same process of evolution, and on a slightly superior social level, we find the Mahilis, Koras and Kurmis, all of whom claim to be members of the Hindu community" (*ibid.*). The Mahilis "appear to have broken off most recently from the tribe (*ibid.*: 77-8). Their close relationship to the Santal seemed to be corroborated in different ways: "They still worship some of the Sonthal gods in addition to the standard Hindu deities; they will eat food cooked by a Sonthal; their caste organization is supervised, like that of the Sonthals, by an official bearing the title of Parganait" (*ibid.*: 78). Their weak integration into the Hindu universe was attested to by the fact that "they have not yet attained to the dignity of employing Brahmans for ceremonial purposes" (*ibid*). *Tribes and Castes of Bengal* offered further examples of their precarious participation in the caste world: "there is no reason to believe", Risley wrote, "that [their headmen and their *panchayat*] have any knowledge of, or pay the smallest regard to, the rules of the regular Hindu law"; their religion is "a mixture of half-forgotten animism and Hinduism imperfectly understood" (1891 b, II: 42).

Fairly extensive information about the Koras is provided in *Tribes and Castes of Bengal*, but in 1866 little was said about them: "there is no clue to warrant their affiliation to any particular tribe (...). They allow adult marriage, their standard of feminine chastity is low, and they have not yet fitted themselves out with Brahmans" (*ibid.*: 78).

Not much more was reported about the Kurmis of West Bengal: they "show signs of a leaning toward orthodox Hinduism, and employ Brahmans for the worship of Hindu gods, but not in the propitiation of their family and rural deities, or in their marriage ceremonies" (*ibid.*).

Table 9 summarizes the classification of the above-mentioned groups:

1. At the bottom of the system: unspecified **non-Aryan groups**, described as

   * having retained their original language;
   * worshipping non-Aryan gods;
   * presenting a "fairly compact tribal organization".

2. At a higher level in the status scale: most **Bhumijs**

   * have lost their original language;
   * worship tribal and Hindu gods;
   * manage to ensure the collaboration of low-class Brahmins.

3. At an even higher level: **Mahilis, Koras** and **Kurmis**, who present considerable divergences:

Mahilis:

   * they appear to be weakly incorporated into the Hindu social system;
   * their religion is seen as a "mixture" of tribal beliefs and poorly assimilated Hindu concepts;
   * they have not yet obtained the religious collaboration of Brahmins.

Koras: * "they have not yet fitted themselves out with Brahmans". **Kurmis**: * they are possibly a Hinduized branch of the Santals; * they have secured the collaboration of Brahmins for a certain number of ritual interventions.

Table 9: *A picture of social precedence according to Risley.*

Do Mahilis, Koras and Kurmis form a coherent group? From the very limited information presented by Risley in 1866 on Koras and Kurmis, it is not possible to grasp the reasons justifying their being placed at the same level of integration into the caste system. Kurmis, perhaps "a Hinduized branch of the Santhals", and Mahilis, whose ancient beliefs combine with a poorly understood Hinduism, inexplicably coexist. The religious conceptions of the Mahilis (level 3) do not differ from those of Bhumijs (level 2). The latter were able to obtain the collaboration of Brahmins, which was not the case for the Mahilis or the Koras (level 3). It is hard to understand why Mahilis and Koras were given a status higher than that of Bhumijs.

At both the "lower" and the "higher" levels, Risley's approach to classification is inconsistent. Social precedence – one of the "independently ascertained" facts called upon to corroborate the statistics of the nasal index – was the product of a rather dubious exercise.

II

Topinard had not been persuaded by Risley's conclusions: "in spite of endogamy", he noted, a long coexistence of populations cannot fail to result in their intermixture (1892: 310).[2] Shortly after his critical remarks were published, others followed. Regretting the absence of a "workable classification of castes", O'Donnell observed that "after his thorough examination of the subject, Mr. Risley has been unable to arrive at any arrangement more effective than an alphabetical list" (1893: 250). And he noted with ill-disguised irony:

> *The figures on which [his thesis] are based are found in the third and fourth volumes of Mr. Risley's instructive work, and if in examining them it appears that they do not bear out his conclusions, I hope not to fail in recognising the great service he has rendered to ethnographic study by introducing really scientific methods of enquiry* (ibid.: 254-55).

As he pointed out, Risley's data on the averages of the nasal index ultimately led to the conclusion "that the Kayastha of Bengal Proper, an undoubtedly Sudra caste, according to Bráhmanic theory, has finer features than the Bráhman, whilst the Chandal outcaste of the Gangetic delta lies midway between the highborn and allied castes of Bráhmans and Babhans in Bihar" (*ibid.*: 255).

O'Donnell aptly compared Risley's views with those of Nesfield, postulating the "unity of the Indian race". Nesfield had noted that "a stranger walking through the class-rooms of the Sanskrit College at Benares would never dream of supposing that the students seated before him were distinct in race and blood from the scavengers, who swept the roads". Perfect confirmation

---

2. "In a recent number of *L'Anthropologie*", Risley wrote nevertheless, "Professor Topinard himself has minutely analised my observations and I am glad to say has drawn from the statistics precisely the same conclusions as I had already formulated in a paper read before the Anthropological Institute of the United Kingdom, in June 1890" (1894: 432-33).

of these views was provided by Risley's anthropometric measurements, which showed after all "no appreciable difference in feature between the Bráhman of the North-Western Provinces and the Chuhra or scavenger of the Panjab". O'Donnell further emphasized that considering "individual measurements" instead of "averages", one was forced to recognize that "the entire absence of any common gradation in the nasal indices of the measured castes is still more apparent" (*ibid.*).

Émile Senart also regarded with suspicion the working hypothesis that Risley intended to convert into an "absolute law": "Who would not remain a little sceptical?" (1896: 199).

In the "Preface" to the first volume of *The Tribes and Castes of the North-Western Provinces and Oudh*, William Crooke reproduced a note on Anthropometry written by Surgeon-Captain H. E. Drake-Brockman. In this note, the social groups under scrutiny were initially divided into three major categories, Aryan, Medium and Dravidian, the last being sub-divided into (a) a Hinduized section and (b) an Aboriginal section, "to indicate more fully their status in the social scale" (1896, I: xxvii). It turned out that the comparison of "the highest with the lowest caste" revealed "very slight material difference(s) (…), a fact which tends to prove beyond doubt that the racial origin of all must have been similar" (*ibid.*: xxxiii).

In short, there was no possible connection between the two orders – social and anthropometric – whose linearity had been artificially forged. But Risley did not abandon his views. On the contrary, he took them up a little later in a new context. Before considering this second phase of his career, however, a pause is necessary.

III

Risley's approach was welcomed by Jervoise Athelstane Baines, the Census Commissioner for 1891, whose general report appeared in 1893: "It is only within comparatively recent times that the racial distribution of the population has been investigated on the line of modern science. (…) A beginning has been made in Bengal by Mr. Risley" (1893: 184). The experiment had been carried out on a small scale but "the results show the value of the method, and it is to be hoped that more material of the same sort may be made available" (*ibid.*).

Baines was primarily interested in the ethnic composition of the subcontinent, but he was by no means indifferent to the question of hierarchy. The theoretical aspect of the problem, however, did not seem to be supported by the concrete reality: he was willing to arrange the castes "more or less in accordance with the position generally assigned to each in the social scale" (*ibid.*: 187) but declared himself unable to do so on the basis of ethnological criteria: "in the *chaotic condition of the population at the present time* an attempt to achieve such would inevitably be a failure" (*ibid.*: 189, italics added).

Even if only in theory, how did Baines conceive a caste hierarchy? Although a gap between "castes" and "occupations" often appeared to be impossible to establish, he did accept the previously assumed separation of the two topics: "Occupation of the Population" (Chapter IV) and "Caste, Tribe, or Race" (section C of Chapter V: "Ethnographic Distribution of the Population").

Attention must be drawn to the way in which Baines successively addressed each of these subjects. He resolutely pointed out the difficulties inherent in occupation-related statistics. The contexts to be examined were so vast and diverse that a high value could not be "attached to the results of the census of occupation" (*ibid.*: 87). Even so, a classification was adopted –

more precisely the classification of Farr, although his name was not mentioned in this context. Instead of the 6 Classes and 18 Orders of the original scheme, 7 Classes divided into 24 Orders and 77 Sub-orders (instead), were now adopted:

Farr's 6 Classes of occupations	Baines' 7 Classes of occupations
• Professional • Domestic • Commercial • Agricultural • Industrial • Indefinite and Non-Productive.	* Government • Pasture and Agriculture • Personal services • The preparation and supply of material substances • Commerce and the Transport of persons, goods and messages, and the storage of goods • Professions, Learned, Artistic and Minor • Indefinite occupations, and means of subsistence independent of occupation.

Table 10: *Classes of occupations (Farr and Baines)*

The similarity between the two schemas is obvious, despite some modifications. Baines' description of Indian reality was based on a historical reconstruction inspired by evolutionary perspectives. It was presumed that every Indian village had been, from the beginning, a self-sufficient agricultural community, able to maintain itself economically and to ensure its protection from the outside world. This explained the preeminent position given to "Pasture and Agriculture".

Baines presumed that the village unit was originally divided into two parts: an "inner circle" composed of the "occupants of the land and the artisans or menials to whom tradition assigns a cognate racial origin"; and a set of lower menials, agrestic serfs, and other groups "whose occupation, in the present day (…), relegates them to an inferior position" (*ibid.*: 94).

This historical "reconstruction" determined, of course, the perception of the world of castes. "Occupations" and "castes" sometimes overlapped and "[i]n some few but important cases, the name of the caste [was] a better indication than that of the principal occupation" (1893: 90). It is therefore not surprising that "castes" and "occupations" were subjected to the same classificatory model:

Farr's Classification of occupations	**Baines' Classification of castes**
• Professional • Domestic • Commercial • Agricultural • Industrial • Indefinite and Non-Productive.	• Agricultural and Pastoral • Professional • Commercial • Artisans and Villlage menials • Vagrants • Race and Indefinite Titles

Table 11: *From "Occupations" to "Castes"*

Compared to Farr's classification model for "occupations", the classification of "castes" proposed by Baines presented a certain number of modifications. The most important, as one might expect, concerned the preeminent place accorded to agriculture and pastoralism.

Castes were distributed as follows:

Agriculture and Pastoral:
Military and Dominant; Other Agriculturists; Cattle Graziers; Field Labourers; Forest Tribes
Professional:
Priests, etc.; Devotees and Ascetics; Temple Servants; Genealogists; Writers; Astrologers and Herbalists; Musicians and

Ballad Reciters; Singers and Dancers; Actors and Mimes

Commercial:

Traders, Pedlars; Carriers by Pack Animals

Artisans and Village Menials:

Goldsmiths; Barbers; Blacksmiths; Carpenters, Masons, etc.; Brass and Copper Smiths; Tailors; Grain Parchers and Confectioners; Perfumers, Betel-leaf, etc. Sellers; Weavers and Dyers; Washermen; Cotton Cleaners; Shepherds and Wool Weavers; Oil Pressers; Potters, Glass and Lac Workers; Salt and Lime Workers; Goldsmiths' Refuse Cleaners; Gold Washers and Iron Smelters; Fishermen, etc.; Domestic Service, etc.; Distillers and Toddy Drawers; Butchers; Leather Workers; Village Watchmen, etc.; Scavengers

Vagrants:

Grindstone Makers; Earth Workers, Stone Quarriers; Knife Grinders; Mat and Cane Workers; Hunters and Fowlers; Miscellaneous Vagrants; Jugglers, Acrobats, etc.

Races and Indefinite Titles:

Musalmán Foreign Races; Himalayan Mongoloids; Burmese and Chinese Mongoloids; Western Asiatics; Burmese, etc. Mixed Races; Indefinite Indian Castes; Europeans, etc.; Eurasians; Native Christians; Goanese and Portuguese; Africans

Table 12: *Classification of "Castes"* (ibid.: 188).

The distribution of castes shown in the Table above was a re-elaboration of Kitts' model, itself a re-elaboration of Farr's scheme. The arrangement proposed by Kitts was not fully respected because Baines had tried to reorganize its groups according to principles which should reflect a social scale which he took "more or less" for granted (*ibid.*: 187). The failure of this attempt is clear. The Class occupying the top position in his list (Agricultural and Pastoral, Table 12) is a heterogeneous one comprising, along with castes of high standing, field labourers who were "in many places but little more than agrestic serfs" (*ibid.*: 189).

The grouping of these castes "is based mainly upon function", the occupation taken into account being "not necessarily that actually exercised by the caste in the present day but that which was assigned to it by tradition" (*ibid.*: 188-89).

The dubious nature of the boundaries between "real" means of livelihood and "traditional" occupations was again underlined here. Why then was it necessary to stress, as Baines did (*ibid.*: 189), that there was "no connection" between the returns concerning both activities? And why should it be considered useful to address them in different chapters of the general report? Were they not submitted, after all, to similar classificatory procedures (as shown in Tables 10 and 11)? Having suggested that both conform to Farr's model (Table 12), Baines implicitly admitted that the caste system itself could be seen in the image of socio-professional relations prevailing in mid-19th century England and Wales…

CHAPTER-6

SOCIAL PRECEDENCE AS CONCEIVED BY PUBLIC OPINION

I

Herbert Hope Risley was appointed Census Commissioner for 1901. Edward Albert Gait – superintendent of the Census of Bengal – assumed the same function in 1902. They co-authored the general report of 1903. Written by Risley, Chapter XI of this work – "Caste, Tribe and Race" – attracted particular attention and influenced later research on the caste system. In this text, the author broadens his previous research and gives it a final expression.

Many other Chapters of the report dealt with old problems and were addressed in terms inherited from previous census operations. As regards "occupations", the model adopted was the one Baines had followed in 1891. But, as always, classification raised enormous embarrassment. The provincial superintendents tirelessly reiterated the difficulties inherent in the process: vagueness and want of precision in the questionnaires were often due to a deficient or incomplete evaluation of the contexts under inquiry.

In Tamil, as W. Francis stressed, "[t]he ordinary vernacular term for the village cobbler is 'Chakkiliyan'" and one could imagine that it would adequately describe a particular occupation.

> *But in the scheme leather-dyers, shoe, boot, and sandal makers, tanners and curriers, sellers of manufactured leather goods, sellers of hides, horns, bristles, and bones, water-bag, well-bag, bucket and ghee pot-makers are all differentiated. The village cobbler is probably any or all of these by turns, and it was not easy to ensure that the entry 'Chakkiliyan' was always consistently classified under the most appropriate of these heads* (1902: 188).

The British officers' inexperience continually threatened the success of the approach: "In Madura (...) eleven persons are returned as receivers of stolen goods. This looked suspicious and the entries were all traced and found to be correctly tabulated". Francis was puzzled: "Whether they accurately represent the facts or are the work of malicious (or facetious) enumerators need not be discussed" (*ibid.*:190).

There were countless examples of activities that, despite their strangeness, Europeans considered appropriate to include in their chapters on "occupations". In Malabar, "there are some hundreds of 'witches, wizards and cow-poisoners'. These are the devil-dancers and sorcerers of that coast, who are classified with witches in default of any more appropriate place for them in the scheme" (*ibid.*).

The provincial reports were teeming with situations revealing the nightmarish nature of the enterprise. The authors were faced with multiple traps: "We had to classify as best we could the various occupations returned which were not covered by any of the entries in the occupation scheme" (Gait 1902: 463). This assertion precedes a vast sequence of apparently unclassifiable returns: "umbrella-repairers, torch-bearers in marriage processions, vendors of Fuller's earth, castrators of animals, makers of wooden sandals, catchers and sellers of snakes, collectors and sellers of the water-weed used for refining sugar" *(ibid.)*.

Many of these testimonies were extensively reproduced in the general report, proving again and again the limited value of inquiries about "occupations" and the frequent impossibility of distinguishing between traditional occupations and "real" means of subsistence. A touch of irony emanated from the mere enumeration of unforeseen activities, accounting for the failure of the classificatory approach. They were more than "simple" illustrations of the misleading nature of the questionnaires and the doubtful conclusions they suggested. What their authors often sought to emphasize was the unbridgeable gap between two ways of seeing and describing the world:

> *The native of South India's idea of the way to fix the time of day at which an event occurred is to say that it happened when the sun was so many palmyra trees high in the heavens, and persons with such rudimentary notions of exactness as this can hardly be expected to give a clear account of their means of subsistence, especially when these are numerous or complex* (Francis 1902: 187).

In other words, Indians did not think like Westerners. The spirit of the 18th century European rhetoric reappears here: India had remained entangled in the past. Her "backwardness" explained the confused mind of the people: "there is throughout India", the general report emphasized, "much confusion of thought between a man's caste, which connotes his traditional occupation, and the means of livelihood by which he actually subsists" (Risley and Gait 1903: 190). It was therefore not enough to separate – for "practical" purposes, as Plowden had done – real means of livelihood from traditional occupations. It appeared incomprehensible that someone who no longer pursued the traditional occupation of his caste still saw in it a mark of personal identity. That was proof of bafflement – and it was in derogatory terms that examples of that attitude were provided:

> *[A] Bráhman, especially if a mendicant, will say he is a priest, even though he may never have exercised any priestly function beyond perhaps dipping his toe in a bowl of water for the delectation of some pious Sudra, who will not break his fast until he has had a draught of water thus sanctified* (ibid.).

II

Risley saw in the census operations of 1901 the opportunity to reinforce the thesis he had formulated ten years earlier. The operations to be carried out would include an ethnological approach, the provincial superintendents being requested to collect information about social precedence *such as conceived by the native public opinion*. Risley believed he could define beforehand the criteria to be considered and, to facilitate the task of the superintendents, gave them the following list:

1. "Particular castes are supposed to be the modern representatives of one or other of the castes of the theoretical Hindu system";
2. "Bráhmans will take water from certain castes";
3. "Bráhmans of high standing will serve particular castes";
4. "Certain castes, though not served by the best Bráhmans, have nevertheless got Bráhmans of their own, whose rank varies according to circumstances";
5. "Certain castes are not served by Bráhmans at all, but have priests of their own";
6. "The status of certain castes has been raised by their taking to infant-marriage or abandoning the remarriage of widows";

7.	"The status of some castes has been lowered by their living in a particular locality";
8.	"The status of others has been modified by their pursuing some occupation in a special or peculiar way";
9.	"Some can claim the services of the village barber, the village palanquin-bearer, the village midwife, etc., while others cannot";
10.	"Some castes may not enter the courtyards of certain temples";
11.	"Some castes are subject to special taboos, such as that they must not use the village well, or may draw water only with their own vessels, that they must live outside the village or in a separate quarter, that they must leave the road on the approach of a high-caste man, or must call out to give warning of their approach".

Table 13: *Criteria for determining "social precedence"* (ibid.: 538).

It is necessary to have a precise idea of the response of most provincial superintendents to Risley's request.

E. A. Gait: Report on the Census of the Lower Provinces of Bengal and their Feudatories (1902).

Gait believed that "under the Hindu *régime* the social precedence of different castes was settled by the monarch himself" (1902: 365). This was a common presupposition about the origin of the principles governing the caste system. Only the monarch could define the precepts concerning the composition of the social body. The author imagined, however, that the essential ideas about the architecture of the system had been lost: "Since the temporal power had passed from the hands of the Hindus first to the Muhammadans and then to the British, there has been no authoritative pronouncement as regards the relative rank of the different castes" (*ibid.*). The Brahmins were seen as custodians of tradition but their standpoint could not express the *public opinion*. Gait concluded that a social hierarchy based on "general acceptance" was not discernible: unanimity was a pure abstraction. When divergence between two groups occurred, the members of each affirmed the superiority of their own community: "no Káyasth would ever admit the superiority of the Baidyas, nor would any Baidya consent to place the Káyasths above his own fraternity". That being the case, it was "very difficult to say precisely what constitutes Hindu public opinion. The Hindus as a body are strangely indifferent to the circumstances of castes that do not clash with their own" (*ibid.*: 366).

A single idea could perhaps generate relative consensus: Brahmins were at the top of the "caste hierarchy" (*ibid.*: 366). But, given the arguments just produced, how could *caste hierarchy* be defined? Nothing relevant was to be inferred from the traditional order of the *varnas*:

> *The conflicting claims of various castes are generally based on their pretensions to take their rank in one or another of [the varnas]. The Káyasths claim to be Kshattriyas, the Chási Kaibarttas to be Vaisyas and so on. (...) Although the general order of these four classes is not disputed, there are numerous degraded sub-castes which occupy a lower status* (ibid.: 366-67).

It seemed impossible to achieve the main goal of the census operations but Gait was not prepared to radically diverge from Risley. This accounts for the striking ambiguity of some of Gait's statements. Members of a caste "of good position", he pointed out, "know very well from whom they can take water and those whose touch defiles, *but they neither know nor care much regarding their relative position*" (ibid.: 366, italics added). Rules concerning acceptance of water were observed *but* no consequences regarding social precedence resulted from them.

This was an inescapable conclusion. Gait was unable to fully comply with Risley's desiderata, but he sought to mask his disaccord: it was "impossible to arrange castes in an order that will command universal acceptance" but there were "well recognised tests (…) by the consideration of which a fairly accurate scale of social precedence [could] be drawn up (*ibid.*: 367)". He was determined to ignore the conflict between the first and last parts of this sentence:

"it is impossible to arrange castes in an order that will command universal acceptance (…)	*[although] a fairly accurate scale of social precedence can be drawn up".*

What was the test that was supposed to resolve Gait's dilemma? "A generally accepted criterion", he wrote, "is whether the higher castes may use water brought by a man of any particular caste or not" (*ibid.*). But Gait had just recognized that it was not possible to infer a scale of social precedence from the acceptance or refusal of water. Strange as it may sound, he did not seem to doubt the effectiveness of the so-called "test of social position", provided by Risley (Table 13).

Gait also observed that a Brahmin "loses in social estimation if he acts as priest to any but those of twice-born rank", adding in the same sentence that "he is not actually degraded for performing the priestly office for persons who are looked upon as clean Sudras" (*ibid.*).

It was well-known that rules adopted in one area were often ignored elsewhere: "In Bengal Proper the Tánti's Bráhman is not degraded, but in Bihar the case is otherwise. The Bhuiyá holds a high position in the Orissa States, but in Bengal Proper, he is unclean". It would therefore be impossible "to frame a single caste precedence list" (*ibid.*: 368). Such facts posed a new threat to Risley's conviction that it would be possible to identify stable (or, at least, relatively stable) positions.

In spite of countless difficulties, tables of precedence continued to be drawn up and submitted to Indians for consideration. Here is an example of what could happen when this procedure was adopted. A tentative list, previously prepared by Risley and later entrusted to Gait, provoked – here as elsewhere – an "extraordinary amount of ill-feeling and jealousy"; Indian committees designated *ad hoc* were powerless to solve the problem. Pointing out that one of those committees had been presided over by a native Judge of the High Court, Gait showed his faith in the ability of privileged informants to decide on matters regarding… "public opinion". But even in such circumstances the results were disappointing: "the animosity between some of the members [of the committee in question] was so pronounced that [the meeting] broke up without arriving at any definite finding (*ibid.*: 369, note).

Conflicts also emerged when the rank of two castes appeared to be "very nearly equal". In such cases, there was "nothing to be gained by attempting to adjudicate between them" (*ibid.*: 369). It would "cause much mortification to the community whose claims were over-ruled; the decision would not be accepted as authoritative, and far from extinguishing, [the attempt] would add fresh fuel to the fires of acrimonious argumentation" (*ibid.*). Special treatment was reserved for such situations: "I have thought it better simply to place the castes in question together, without making any assertion as to their individual position in the group in which they are classed" (*ibid.*).

Even more serious difficulties awaited the superintendent with regard to the seven groups into which he distributed the population of Bengal Proper (*ibid.*: 369-372):

I. Brahmins
II. Other castes ranking above clean Shudras
III. Clean Shudras
IV. Clean castes with degraded Brahmins
V. Castes lower than the above whose water is not usually taken
VI. Low castes who abstain from beef, pork and fowls
VII. Unclean feeders.

Table 14: *The seven groups of castes of Bengal Proper.*

The characterization of these groups and the arrangement of castes inside each of them obeyed poorly defined criteria.

I. The first group is introduced by using a formula with a general scope: "In Bengal Proper, as in all other parts of the province, and of India generally, the Bráhman stands without cavil on the top rung of the social ladder". But alongside high- standing Brahmins, many others are found with a low or very low status: those who serve as priests to the Káyasths and the Nabasákha "suffer somewhat in public estimation"; the same happens with those "who act as cooks, bakers, confectioners, hired worshippers of family idols and the like"; those "who serve castes ranking below the Navasákhas (...) are degraded. They will eat *kachchi* food [ordinary food] in the houses of their respective *jajmáns*, *i.e.*, of the persons whom they serve as priests"; the higher castes refuse water from them – and we read, not without surprise, that "they rank below group IV" and that "their rank varies according to the castes whom they serve". Particularly vulnerable is the status of the Piráli, "who are said to owe their low position to having been forced to smell or, as some say, eat, the cooked food of a Muhammadan" (*ibid.*: 369).

II. "The Khatris and Rájputs or Chattris stand at the top of the second group, but neither of these are, strictly speaking, Bengal castes" (*ibid.*). They are followed by Baidya and Káyasth, each claiming to be of higher status than the other. The Ugra Kshatriya occupies the bottom, and "several of the district committees recommended his relegation to Group III" (*ibid.*: 370).

III. The third group includes those commonly considered clean Shudras, "whose water is taken by the higher castes, and who are served by good Bráhmans". The Navasákhas are among them. "The relative rank of the castes in this group varies in different parts of the country" but the difference between them "is so slight that it is impossible to draw any hard-and-fast dividing line between [them]". They are arranged in alphabetical order (*ibid.*).

IV. The fourth group contains just two castes, Chási Kaibartta and Goálá. Higher castes accept water from their hands; their Brahmin is degraded. The reasons why Gait claimed they form a "well defined" group, are not clear. In fact, high castes *do not accept* water from the members of some Goálá sub-castes; and, in some districts, the Brahmin who serves the Goálá is *not degraded*.

V. The criteria that are used to form the fifth Group are surprising: the castes gathered here "have little or nothing in common with each other", their juxtaposition being "due to the fact that they all rank below the castes already enumerated" (*ibid.*: 371). They are indexed alphabetically.

VI. Gait "combined in group VI a number of castes that, in [a] original draft, were distributed over four separate groups". They are indeed very different from each other: "the various committees differed so widely as to their relative position that it was found impossible [to harmonize their views]" (*ibid.*). The castes arrangement "as usual is alphabetical" (*ibid.*: 372).

VII. The last Group is made up of "unclean feeders", about whom nothing is said. They are also alphabetically presented.

W. Francis: Report on the Census of Madras Presidency (1902).

According to Francis, a "scientific classification" of castes required the collaboration of different disciplines. But he doubted that anthropometry could help to distinguish "the very many semi-Dravidian castes of which the bulk of the population consists" (1902: 126). He thought that the basic principles of the caste system were too unstable to be comprehensible: marriage and commensality prescriptions differed "in every district, and almost in every taluk". In the case of large castes, "mutually exclusive groups [were] (...) changing every day", forming "a most perplexing and unstable foundation for any scientific scheme of classification" (*ibid.*). The elaboration of a mere glossary would be a Sisyphean task: no one could ever complete it "for the reason that, by the time he had worked down to the castes at the end of the alphabet, changes would have taken place in the practices of those at the beginning of it" (*ibid.*: 128).

Although stressing the impossibility of a coherent definition of the caste structure, Francis did not openly reject Risley's views. Like Gait, he evoked Risley's "tests":

> *Social estimation can be gauged by the degree to which the food and water touched by the various castes will be accepted by others (...); by their occupations; by their wearing or not wearing the sacred thread; by their allowing or not allowing infant marriage and widow re-marriage; and by the distance within which they are permitted to approach the innermost part of the temples* (ibid.: 129).

In a table "drawn up at the direction of the Census Commissioner", fourteen sets – *sets* again, instead of *castes* individually considered – were arranged as follows:

I.	Bráhman and allied castes
II.	Kshatriya and allied castes
III.	Vaisya and allied castes
IV.	Sat-Súdras or Good Súdras
V.	Súdras who habitually employ Bráhmans as puróhits and whose touch pollutes to a slight degree
VI.	Súdras who occasionally employ Bráhmans as puróhits and whose touch pollutes
VII.	Súdras who do not employ Bráhmans as puróhits and whose touch pollutes
VIII.	Castes which pollute even without touching but do not eat beef
IX.	Castes which eat beef but do not pollute except by touch
X.	Castes which eat beef and pollute even without touching
XI.	Castes which deny the sacerdotal authority of the Bráhmans
XII.	Cases in which caste was insufficiently indicated
XIII.	Castes foreign to the Presidency
XIV.	Castes not stated

Table 15: *Groups of castes by social precedence* (ibid.: 136).

These sets were a compromise. The aims of the Census Commissioner were unattainable. The traditional *varna* system – groups I-IV in the table – had only in theory been accepted in South India. The bottom of the list was occupied by castes whose very low status raised no doubts. But the remaining ones – representing the majority of the population – were unclassifiable: "much difficulty was experienced in finding criteria and touchstones which would apply throughout all grades of society in all parts of the Presidency" (*ibid.*:129). The original draft of this list of sets was submitted for consideration to "committees of native gentlemen", and it was "criticised and amended" (*ibid.*: 130); but unanimity had not been reached.

The difficulties of the task did not differ after all from those arising from the classification of groups in English society: "Princes and peers would clearly come first, and costermongers and coal-heavers last, but to decide the relative precedence of the butcher, the baker and the candlestick-maker, or of the solicitor, the doctor and the schoolmaster, would tax the discretion of the most experienced of Lord Chamberlains" (*ibid.*).

H. A. Rose: Report on the Punjab, its Feudatories, and the North-West Frontier Province (1902).

An arrangement of castes according to Risley's principles was considered out of reach: "The attempt to classify castes in the order of their social precedence was (...) doomed to failure from the outset". The difficulty arose, in the first place, from the protean character of each group. In Rose's opinion, "Hindu society may be divided (...) into two main grades, the clean and the unclean, but beyond that no social classification of the castes appears to be possible" (*ibid.*: 337).

A. D. Bannerman: Report on Rajputana (1902)

Wishing to achieve a classification of castes "by social precedence as recognised by native public opinion", Bannerman hastened to send a copy of Risley's request to local advisors. They immediately noted that "the subject was a delicate and difficult matter to deal with", the borderline between certain groups being "very faint".

To overcome the acknowledged obstacles, the superintendent though it would be wise to resort to the "tests" of the Census Commissioner; but when the replies were received "it was found that in some statements the grouping of the castes varied very considerably and that castes which had been assigned a high position in some lists had been accorded a relatively low place in others" (1902: 131). Bannerman did his best to meet Risley's expectations but had to admit that, in the final analysis, the results proved unsuccessful.

R. V. Russell: Report on the Census of Central Provinces (1902)

Russel did not think that community of race rather than community of function was the key principle of the caste system: "differences of occupation seem to be the principal basis of caste distinctions". This did not prevent him from arranging the castes "according to social status (...) under the instructions of the Census Commissioner" (*ibid.*: 158).

Five groups were defined by direct reference to Risley's list (Table 13, points 1, 2, 10, 11): the first included descendants from the three higher *varnas* and a "few others who have obtained a specially high position on account of the sanctity or importance of their occupation"; the second division comprised castes from whom Brahmins accepted water; the third group was made up of those from whom Brahmins refused water but allowed access to Hindu temples; the last two included Dravidian tribes to which different degrees of impurity were attributed. Russell was sceptical about the results obtained:

> *Within each group there are further differences of status; but as prolonged inquiry would have been necessary to ascertain these exactly, and as they vary greatly in different parts of the provinces, it has been thought better not to attempt any more elaborate sub-division. Even the classification given above proceeds partly on fiction* (ibid.: 158-59).

R. E. Enthoven: Report on the Census of Bombay Presidency (1902)

In Enthoven's words, "There is perhaps no subject within

the proper scope of an Indian Census Report that presents more difficulties, or is beset with greater uncertainty, than that which confronts the writer when he approaches the classification of the people by caste and tribe" (1902: 174). Like so many other authors, he recalled the impossibility of finding an acceptable answer to the eternal question: "What is a caste?" To this question, asked by an enumerator, "the Indian householder is apt to reply by giving a trade, a sect, a name of a locality, or even a proper name" (*ibid.*: 174-75). And he added: "Possibly he has no very clear notion of the significance of the term at all" (*ibid.*: 175). This all made the task required by the Census Commissioner impossible:

> *An attempt to classify the people on a caste basis is (...) tantamount to entering on a discussion concerning the real nature of caste, which, as an amorphous collection of anomalies and anachronisms, is calculated to puzzle the most expert enquirer, if not to deter the most ardent enthusiast in search of a scientific classification of the people* (ibid.).

No arrangement seemed satisfactory: an alphabetical list brought together groups with nothing in common; "the composition of a warrant of precedence (…) [was] open to numerous objections" – namely "the unpopularity which it brings to any Superintendent who is sufficiently venturesome to attempt it" (*ibid.*: 188).

N. Subramhanya Aiyar: Report on the Census of Travancore (1903)

Subramhanya Aiyar endeavoured to conduct his research in the spirit of Risley's request:

> *At the instance of the Census Commissioner for India, a memo of points to be considered in determining the order of precedence, along with a series of*

> *ethnographic questions, was prepared and circulated by Government among a number of persons competent to form an opinion on the subject. A provisional list was also framed to serve as a basis to proceed upon* (1903: 257).

The results of this process were as follows: "Out of 111 persons to whom the list and questions were sent, replies were received from 26 and of these, only 6 felt prepared to offer views on the question of precedence" (*ibid.*). The procedure needed to obtain a "precedence list" was ultimately "a slippery undertaking" (*ibid.*: 258).

T. Ananda Row: Report on the Census of Mysore (1903)

Similar remarks were produced regarding Mysore. In Ananda Row's words, among the different operations related to the "abstraction of Census statistics", none involved more difficulties and uncertainties than the classification of castes:

> *The ramifications of castes and sub-castes have already become so widespread and plaited, that in the stupendous growth the base and the main trunk have, in several cases, been altogether lost sight of, so that is now by no means easy either to distinguish the branch from the trunk and the twig from the branch and sometimes even to locate the root of any trunk, branch or twig* (1903: 489).

Hence, no attempt had been made to subordinate castes "to any scheme of social precedence". In the present state of society castes had "multiplied almost indefinitely" and it would not be possible to assign any of them a precise place; nor was "any common principle of precedence recognised by the people themselves by which to grade the Castes" (*ibid.*: 490). It had been suggested by some authors "that the status of Castes varies in relation to a variety of considerations, such as widow marriage, peculiarities of occupation (...), locality and so forth. Perhaps, it does. But which is higher than the other, it is difficult to say" (*ibid.*)

III

Risley rejoiced at "the general success" of his experiment. Almost all superintendents "readily grasped the main idea of the scheme, and their patient industry, supplemented by the intelligent assistance readily given by the highest native authorities, has added very greatly to our knowledge of an obscure and intricate subject" (*ibid.*: 538). He no longer doubted the coherence of a social precedence derived from "native public opinion". But his attitude was possible only in so far as he completely silenced the scepticism of the provincial superintendents. We have noted how profuse the passages of the provincial superintendents were concerning the theme of "occupations"; how insistent they had been about the difficulties inherent in the classification of means of livelihood. Their comments were taken seriously and abundantly reproduced in the general report of 1903. But nothing of the sort happened in relation to the generalized "failure" of the superintendents' search for a "social precedence as conceived by public opinion"...

Defending the plausibility of his perspectives at all costs, Risley became entangled in a web of flimsy arguments. Consider the following example.

The dissatisfaction caused among Indians by the British "tables of precedence" had often been acknowledged. Similar reactions were triggered in 1881, when Plowden attempted a classification of castes "by social position" (1883: 277). He resolutely abandoned that project: he was unable to understand the Indians' discomfort. But Risley arrived at different conclusions: "the great number of petitions and memorials" (*ibid.*: 539) he had received were undeniable proof of the validity of his theses:

> *If the principle on which the classification was based had not appealed to the usages and traditions of the great mass of Hindus, it is inconceivable that so many people should have taken much trouble and incurred substantial expenditure with the object of securing its application in a particular way* (ibid.).

The Khatris, a trading caste of the Panjab and North-west India, gave him the opportunity to better illustrate his point. They had refused to be classified as Vaishyas (as referred to in the Bengal census report of 1891) since a table circulated by Risley himself had equated their status to that of the Rajputs. Authorities had even been called on to ascertain their rights: they "descended from the Kshatriyas of Hindu mythology, much as if the modern Greeks were to claim direct descent from Achilles and were to cite the Catalogue of the Ships in support of their pretentions" (*ibid.*).

Risley did not make much of the arguments produced by the Khatris. What really interested him were the criteria on which the structure of the census could be based: "*For census purposes* the fact that most people do hold this belief was sufficient in itself, and it would have been irrelevant to enquire into the grounds upon which the opinion was based" (*ibid.*: 539, italics added).

In fact, the Khatris' reaction said nothing about their position in a possible social ladder. Gait had already pointed out that indications regarding the social precedence of castes could not be withdrawn from the theoretical order of the *varnas* (1902: 367). Each *varna* included degraded groups but this was to be dismissed.

***

In Risley' words, castes could only be classified "on the basis of social precedence" (*ibid.: 557*). But he *did not present* them in the order he deemed correct. Large classes were formed, the castes being placed inside each of those classes "in alphabetical order so as to escape the necessity of settling the more delicate questions of precedence" (*ibid.*: 540). This was an unexpected decision, supported by an even more unexpected justification: social precedence was a "delicate question"!

The "large classes" just referred to were those presented by Gait in 1902 in his report on the *Census of the Lower Provinces of Bengal* (*see* Table 14). An alphabetical arrangement had been adopted, as previously explained, simply because *no other system had proven possible*. Risley's story was different: supposedly revealed by laboriously framed tables, the precedence of castes had to remain hidden from the Indians themselves. Strangely enough, the expression of their *public opinion* could not be *publicly* declared... Quarrels over relative positions were feared and Risley found it advisable to avoid the problem: the presumed *mutual consent* was, after all, a cause of unsolvable dispute.

IV

The ethnographic inquiry undertaken as part of the 1901 census was not based on anthropometry. Conducted in a short period, it obviously excluded anthropometric measurements. But the correspondence previously postulated between the statistics of nasal index and a presumptive social scale extrapolated from public opinion, seemed to authorize a conclusion. Similar results would be obtained by choosing to use one or the other of two methods: anthropometric measurements *or* a survey of public opinion.

Social precedence and racial theory had been presented in 1891 as inextricable aspects of the same argument, the former having proved essential to the reliability of the latter. C. J. Fuller admits, however, that social precedence "can easily be separated from the racial theory" and that, "in the long run it mattered far more for the study of caste" (2016: 233).

Let us add that, still according to Fuller, Risley would have been unfairly interpreted: "To make sense of Risley's approach to race (…) we have to look at it in its own historical context and examine it with more dispassionate accuracy than his later-day critics have normally displayed". (2024: 134). In fact, historical perspectives alone do not provide a better understanding of the ideas being discussed. The very inconsistency of Risley's arguments was promptly acknowledged by his contemporaries.

Fuller further argues that, at the time when Risley had been appointed Census Commissioner, he had abandoned his earlier views on racial theory. He now referred to "physical types" – which, although "defined in relation to race, (…) were not themselves 'races' or 'racial types'" (*ibid.*: 114). By 1901, we are told, he had changed his mind: "he was thinking about race much more like a modern social scientist, for whom it is always a social and cultural construct, not a physical or biological fact" (*ibid.*: 264).

This is unacceptable. The Census Commissioner did not deviate in any way from his perspectives of 1891. At no time did he abandon his former belief in the probative value of the nasal index: the distinctive feature of the physical type, he wrote again in 1903, "the character which gives the real clue to its origin and stamps the Aryo-Dravidian as racially different from the Indo-Aryan, is to be found in the proportions of the nose" (1903: 503).

The Chapter *Caste, Tribe and Race* of the general report began precisely by praising Anthropometry, and then long passages by Topinard were reproduced almost literally. Risley also recalled the role he himself had played in the introduction of scientific anthropometry in India. The event had a precise date: it had taken place "seventeen years ago" (*ibid.*: 493) – the date of the publication of *Primitive Marriage in Bengal*.

Risley persisted in ignoring the criticisms to which his work had been subjected. New anthropometric measurements had since been carried out in different parts of the country, always supported by a presumed social precedence. The arguments produced in 1903 were exactly those of 1891. The opposition between the Indo-Aryan and Dravidian types was taken up in the general report in the terms previously defined:

> *The typical Dravidian (...) has a nose as broad in proportion to its length as the Negro, while this feature in the Indo-Aryan group can fairly bear comparison with the noses of sixty-eight Parisians, measured by Topinard (...). Even more striking is the curiously close correspondence between the gradations of racial type indicated by the nasal index and certain of the social data ascertained by independent inquiry* (ibid.: 498).

The old racial presuppositions remained unaltered: wherever it was possible to report a strong Dravidian presence it was "scarcely a paradox to lay down as *a law of the caste organization* that the social status of the members of a particular group varies in inverse ratio to the mean relative width of their noses" (*ibid.*, italics added). The law of "concomitant variation", formerly evoked as a "working hypothesis", was now reiterated, without the slightest hesitation.

Risley 1891: 253	**Risley and Gait 1903: 498**
Take the fifteen castes of Bengal Proper, the two castes of Behar, the seventeen castes of Chota Nagpore, and the twenty-three castes of the North-West Provinces for which this index has been measured, arrange them in the order of the nasal	If we take a series of castes in Bengal, Bihar, the United Provinces of Agra and Oudh, or Madras, and arrange them in the order of the average nasal index, so that the caste with the finest nose shall be at the top, and that with the coarsest at the bottom of the list,

index, putting the lowest or most leptorhine index at the top, and it will be found that the order thus arrived at corresponds substantially with the order of social precedence.	it will be found that this order substantially corresponds with the accepted order of social precedence.

Presuming that, at the dawn of the 20th century, Risley had abandoned his former conceptions, Fuller cannot understand why the "notorious claim about the nasal index and social status" was reproduced (in fact, even reinforced!) in the general report of 1903 (and in *The People of India*):

> *It is particularly unfortunate that Risley misled his readers (...) by not fully revising his text to make it clear that he had modified his own earlier theory of caste and race. After all, his notorious claim about the nasal index and social status was even less convincing in the context of his new arguments than it had been earlier, but he reiterated it all the same* (Fuller 2024: 275).

It was in no way due to "unfortunate" negligence that Risley alluded in his latest texts to his famous "sociological law". After having reaffirmed – both in 1903 and 1908 – the "concomitant variation" between social status and relative width of noses, he added: "Nor is this the only point in which the two sets of observations – the social and the physical – bear out and illustrate each other" (1903: 498; 1915 [1908]: 29). The nature of the exogamous sections "also varies in a definite relation to the gradations of physical type" (*ibid.*). The strict dichotomy of his old conceptions re-emerged here in complete clarity: "Within a certain range of nasal proportions, [exogamous units] are based almost exclusively on the totem. Along with a somewhat finer form of nose", different groups are found – castes whose exogamous sections are represented by "the eponymous saints and heroes who in India, as in Greece and Rome, are associated with a certain stage of Aryan progress" (*ibid.*). Risley was referring here, of course, to the conclusions of his 1886 article, *Primitive Marriage in Bengal*.

CHAPTER-7
ARBITRARY RULES OF METHOD

I

Célestin Bouglé, a disciple of Émile Durkheim, published in *L'Année Sociologique* (1900) an article under the title *Remarques sur le régime des castes*, later included in *Essais sur le régime des castes* (1908) (*Essays on the Caste System*).

This was sometimes considered to be one of the works that allowed Risley's perspectives to be included in the field of Sociology. But the sociological specificity of the book is debatable. As W. Paul Vogt noted, Bouglé was "obviously horrified by the caste system". Unlike many scholars of the Durkheimian tradition – Marcel Mauss and Marcel Granet, among others – he found nothing "to admire in the non-Western society he studies" (1979: 133).

Robert Parkin sought to moderate Vogt's view. In his opinion, Bouglé, a "quite independent-minded Durkheimian", had written the *Essays* as "a test of the validity" of an earlier book, *Les Idées égalitaires* (Parkin 2002: 115). The nature of this test – which had the explicit purpose of opposing Indian hierarchy and Western egalitarianism – is precisely the most problematic aspect of Bouglé's work. "My desire", he declared in 1908, "was not to imagine *a priori* but to research into the ins and outs of a system that was the most contrary to that which egalitarian ideas are establishing in the west" (1971 [1908]: 5). His main goal was to draw an antithesis between two extreme types of society. "The progress of our civilization drags us towards egalitarianism", he claimed in *Les Idées égalitaires*: (1899: 237, our translation); the opposite happened in India: "the idea which is most repugnant to the [Indian] law (…) is most certainly the idea of the equality of men before the law" (1971: 123).

Through the systematic inversion of the ideal Western conception, the author converted India into a dystopian world. All his arguments were intended to create a radical opposition between India and the West; all aimed, in other words, at highlighting the negative features of Hindu society.

India only served Bouglé's purpose insofar as she could be described as *unique*. Here is the author's first question: "Is the caste system a universal phenomenon common to all civilizations or is it a unique phenomenon peculiar to India?" (*ibid.*: 7). Different opinions – those of Dubois, Max Müller, Crooke, Senart and Risley – were declared unsatisfactory. A consistent vision could only be attained if three major principles – "repulsion", "hierarchy" and "hereditary specialization" – were considered together (*ibid.*: 9). A society is organized according to a caste system if it comprises a "large number of mutually opposed groups which are hereditarily specialized and hierarchically arranged" (*ibid.*).

From what concrete examples was it possible to draw such a general rule? The very alternative as to the characteristics of the caste system – a single occurrence or a universal phenomenon – suggested that the proposed "integral definition" was sufficiently generalized to be relevant in a variety of cases. But the author promptly noted that the scope of his definition was quite restricted: "If there are few civilizations into which one or other of [the three tendencies in question] has not penetrated, there are also few in which all three united are to be seen flourishing freely" (*ibid.*: 11).

What were those societies? No response was given. Ancient Egypt, classical Greece and even Medieval Europe (*ibid.*: 12-16) did not illustrate Bouglé's definition. In fact, only Hindu society met the specified criteria: "Hereditary specialization, hierarchical organization, reciprocal repulsion: as far as any social form can realize itself in its purity, the caste system is realized in India". The author insisted, without factual evidence, that the three principles together play "some part in other civilizations", but only in India had they "invaded the whole"; "in this sense" – he concluded – "we may speak of the caste system as a phenomenon peculiar to India" (*ibid.*: 27).

A "general rule" which only applies to a single occurrence is not general at all. We face a circular reasoning here. Imaginary features of an imaginary Hindu society were converted into elements of a pattern only fully recognized… in that imaginary instance.

***

India was by no means the only fictitious object Bouglé dealt with: the egalitarian Western society was itself, of course, a totally imaginary reality projected in a totally imaginary future.

Western societies, as depicted in *Les idées égalitaires*, were driven towards permanent improvement. Conceived as an embodiment of this upward movement, the ideal European worker, "the worker of the future (*le travailleur idéal, le travailleur de l'avenir*)", would always be ready to change his profession: mobility was the *sine qua non* of a progress-oriented world (1898: 234). India, on the contrary, was immersed in the backward state of a distant past: the caste system had allowed the country to abandon barbarism but from then on "further growth (had been) prevented" (1971: 131). In this regard, Bouglé echoed James Mill, partially reproduced by Irving: the institution of caste had led the nation to "a moderately high pitch of civilization", and after that, "when manual dexterity had arrived at its limit", attempts at further progress were discouraged (1853: 64; 66).

Bouglé did not merely stress the country's primitivism. He thought that India, moving backwards, "prolonged, indefinitely, a phase that other civilizations have only passed through – or rather, she, like the others has developed the primitive principles but *in an inverse direction* to the general one" (1971: 61, italics added). Rather than just manifesting an "arrested sociological development", India illustrated an unexpected reversal of the civilizational trajectory. Her absolute singularity was revealed by history itself.

***

Bouglé did not have any first-hand knowledge of India. But the sources he chose and the way they were used testify to the result he desired for his whole project.

Matthew Atmore Sherring, a protestant missionary often quoted in the *Essays*, had observed that the institution of caste divided, and irremediably separated, the Indian people (1881: 276). Relationships in everyday life were infused with "the poison of deadly strife", giving rise to "enmity between neighbours on the most trivial grounds". Caste was at the root of social anarchy. Its rules exercised "the strongest power of disintegration the human race has ever been subjected to" (*ibid.*: 218):

> *What shall we say of the two hundred and fifty millions inhabiting India, who have chosen to separate themselves from one another for a multitude of reasons (...) – reasons arising from difference of occupation, from religious feeling, from social interests, from a love of superiority, from selfishness, from caprice, from arrogance, from a spirit of exclusiveness, from eating certain things and not eating others, from adopting certain usages and not adopting others?* (ibid.: 219).

The complete absence of connection between groups had made India unique, the missionary had already stated: "no such system of national dismemberment (...) has ever prevailed in any other country" (*ibid.*: 217). The Hindus were a "disunited people, with mutual antipathies and non-resemblances, instead of mutual likenesses and mutual concord" (*ibid.*: 234). Feelings of reciprocal execration dominated the Indian way of life. Brahmins, in particular, were depicted as men whose "monstruous arrogance, selfishness and assumption have proved the bane of their race" (*ibid.*); but it was also believed that the "infatuation of pride, self-esteem, and exclusiveness penetrates all the castes" (*ibid.*: 236).

The French sociologist adopted these conceptions. Other authors, also read and quoted, had departed from such views. Jogendra Nath Bhattacharya, President of the Nadia College of Pandits, pointed out that most of the "inconsistencies" and "fallacies" of the missionary were "too obvious to require any critical exposition"; but he did denounce some of them: "generally speaking, there does not exist that antipathy between the several castes which the world at large has been led to believe" (1896: 3). As he noted, "There is, upon the whole, no more animosity between a Rajput and a Brahman than between a Rajput and a Rajput, or between a Brahman and a Brahman". Hindus consider "the several divisions in their society as the necessary component parts of their social mechanism, and there can be no occasion for jealousy or bitter feelings" (*ibid.*: 4). But it was Sherring's, not Bhattacharya's point of view, that supported the argument of the *Essays*. Sherring's opinion, according to which India was under "the most active principle of disintegration that the world has ever known" (Bouglé 1971: 142) seemed undisputable. An imperative need for differentiation led to permanent antipathy. Society was composed of groups that "repel each other rather than attract" (*ibid.*: 9), elements "eternally closed to one another" (*ibid.*: 24), "social micro-organisms" dominated by fear of "being degraded by mixing" (*ibid.*: 83). Hindus of different castes were "foreigners to each other" (*ibid.*: 23). Described as an "inorganic mass" (*ibid.*: 54), the Indian world of the *Essays* is indeed sociologically unthinkable.

The extreme fragmentation of Hindu society was for Bouglé synonymous with primitivism. His conception of "primitivism", however, was not supported by Durkheimian perspectives. According to *The Division of Labour in Society*, primitive societies were composed of tightly united elements, juxtaposed as "rings of an earthworm". A particular form of solidarity ("mechanical solidarity" in Durkheim's terminology) stemmed from the *similarity* of such elements (1933: 176-77). It was accepted that *any* division of labour, however embryonic it might be, would be based on a network of functional interdependencies. No doubt, dissimilarities of a certain kind could also be a means of cohesiveness. Each segment, Durkheim acknowledged, has "its own features and is thereby distinguished from others" (*ibid.*: 177). A combination of similarities *and* differences was thus postulated: "according to the societies, the two contrary necessities are satisfied in different proportions, but the social type remains the same" *(ibid.)*. It was understood that the social type in question (characterized by segmental organization) *remains the same* if – and only if – "similarities" prevail over "differences". Bouglé moved away from this principle. He certainly saw Hindu society as a "juxtaposition" of "elementary collectivities" (*ibid.*: 141); but while Durkheim insisted on the prevalence of similarities, Bouglé stressed differences – not differences leading to complementarity and collaboration but radical differences, leading to distrust and avoidance. Artificially abstracted from the network of relationships, each caste was seen as "a very simple social type" (*ibid.*), an elementary collectivity with minimal internal differentiations. It corresponded to the homogeneous entity conceived by Durkheim as "the true social protoplasm", while the caste system as a whole was the sum of isolated and hostile entities – a society exclusively founded on antagonism:

Primitive society (Durkheim):	**India as a primitive society (Bouglé):**
Juxtaposition of *similar* elements	Juxtaposition of *different* elements
Similarity leading to reciprocal integration	Irreducible oppositions: a threat of social disintegration
Mechanical solidarity	Absence of solidarity
Attraction	Repulsion

Table 16: *Primitive society: Bouglé versus Durkheim.*

II

Durkheim had opposed "modern" and "primitive" societies. The former showed a highly diversified specialization, its constituent groups being united by powerful bonds of *organic solidarity*; the latter presented an incipient division of labour, its different groups being brought together by *mechanical solidarity*. Under which of these two types should Hindu society be classified? It had developed an extreme professional specialization in spite of the negative features imputed to it (fragmentation, isolation of castes, antipathy, mutual repulsion). Primitive but highly specialized, it was not just an expression of resistance to the analytical frame of the Durkheimian typology. It was a pure paradox.

Bouglé could not fail to recognize the obstacles that had to be transposed: "What are the distinctive forms, conditions and consequences of a division of labour that goes hand in hand with the parceling out of a society in little groups, jealously closed?" (*ibid.*: 156). Although he declared his affiliation with the Durkheimian school, he concluded that the caste system escaped once and for all the categorizations of Durkheim. In the words of a well-known passage from *The Division of Labour*, "Those who resemble assemble" but "those who differ complement each other". Bouglé quoted it to show that it could not be applied in India. Similarities and convergence? Differences and complementarity? Such results can certainly be produced by the division of labour:

> *But (...) for this happy influence to be experienced it is necessary that it be not contradicted by the general current of the social system. If the latter works to deepen the trenches between the collaborating groups, the moral benefit of collaboration is lost. Which is precisely what has happened in India* (ibid.: 169).

Solidarity, one of the most important effects of the division of labour, was inconceivable in the Hindu context: "too many traditional scruples, too much instinctive disdain separates the members of the different castes for them to think of treating each other as collaborators" (*ibid.*). Preposterous as it may sound, collaboration here was chimerical.

Division of labour without collaboration was a Gordian knot. To find a way out, Bouglé deemed it necessary to redefine the concept: "It is sometimes said that the division of labour is the very soul of caste organization. (…) But what kind of labour are we talking about?" (*ibid.*: 156). The question was intended to stress, once again, the disaccord between India and Europe:

> *We mean by division of labour the creation of new specializations: we pre-suppose a sufficient degree of social mobility as to allow individuals, not hesitating to change their occupations, to turn towards the newly created specializations* (ibid.: 165-66).

One still did not see how professional specialization had developed without social collaboration. But that was no longer the main question. *Mobility* and *innovation* were now the decisive criteria for an accurate definition of the division of labour, the means of an improvement inaccessible to the Hindu world (*ibid.*: 166): "the specialized caste keeps its members immobile" (*ibid.*: 141). India had produced an astonishing diversity of specializations but *not* a... true division of labour.

***

The emergence of individualism had also been seen by Durkheim as a result of the division of labour in modern societies. Regarding Hindu society, Bouglé's conclusions were predictable: "No system could be conceived more suited to check the effects normally to be expected of the division of labour. Tied up in its own sacred threads it is incapable either of weaving a new solidarity out of the social segments that it has specialized, or of opening new fields for the scope of individuality" (*ibid.*: 167).

For the same reasons, inventiveness was devalued. The talent of the Hindu artisan could not be ignored: he produced masterpieces using "poor industrial equipment". But masterpieces obtained with rudimentary means aroused scepticism: "We may conjecture what price is paid for such perfection" (*ibid.* 165).

According to Durkheim, the division of labour in modern societies produced:	**According to Bouglé, the Indian "division of labour" did not:**
complementarity and mutual attraction	avoid mutual repulsion
social solidarity	prevent social disintegration
functional interdependencies	produce functional interdependencies
individualism.	produce individualism

Table 17: *Individualism denied: Bouglé versus Durkheim.*

Bouglé alluded to the writings of Mahadev Govind Ranade to better show how Hindu economic life differed from classical Western economics (*ibid.*: 143). Earlier Western theorists, Ranade had begun by noting, believed their assumptions were "as universally true as the First law of Mechanics, that bodies move in straight lines" (1906 [1898]: 8). They assumed, among other things,

1. that a national economy is essentially individualistic;
2. that the individual, or typical Economical man, has no desire but that of promoting his own self-interest;
3. that this self-interest is best promoted by the largest production of wealth, *i.e.,* articles with value in exchange, at the least trouble;
4. that such pursuit of private gain by each individual promotes best the general good, etc. (*ibid.*: 9).

Ranade further observed that such assumptions were largely irrelevant in India: "Self-interest in the shape of the desire of wealth is not absent, but it is not the only or principal motor. The pursuit of wealth is not the only ideal aimed at". In India, "an average individual man is, to a large extent, the very antipodes of the economical man. The family and the caste are more powerful that the individual in determining his position in life" (*ibid.*: 10).

These considerations had not the slightest impact on Bouglé's thinking – or rather, they were turned against Ranade and used to support the thesis of the *Essays* (Bouglé 1971: 168).

III

When Bouglé published what would become the first part of the *Essays*, Risley's work – Bouglé's only source on caste hierarchy[1] – had already been harshly criticized. C. J. O'Donnell had firmly condemned the methods of anthropometry and denounced the probative character of Risley's results: "It appears from the nasal statistics that not only an occasional Bráhman, but a very appreciable section of the caste, may be as flat faced as a Chamar" (1893: 256).

Bouglé ignored these remarks, just as Risley had done. Limiting himself to a discreet reference to the new anthropometric measurements published by Crooke, he simply noted that Risley's thesis rested "upon a manifest exaggeration". Inferences from the data had been overstated, but that was of no real importance. Although it was not possible "to distinguish *with certainty* brahmins from other castes" (Bouglé 1900: 59, note 5, italics added), the racial theory should not be rejected. One could assume that present day social and moral differences must have corresponded in the past to clear physical variations (*ibid.*: 57-8).

Bouglé refrained from reproducing the figures published by Crooke. Unable to accept that they really did imply the collapse of Risley's ideas, he tried the best he could to conceal the vulnerability of his racial thesis. And in spite of the fact that this

---

1. In order to proclaim the hierarchy of castes, Bouglé began by quoting a passage by Dubois, alluding to the supreme selfishness of the Brahmins: "are they not brought up to believe that all is owing to them and that they owe nothing?" (1971: 21). Dubois had observed next that the Brahmins' "absolute superiority is as uncontested as the absolute inferiority of the Pariahs" and Bouglé concluded that "between these two extremes the great multitude of castes are arranged in their different degrees, each one preoccupied to hold its rank and to preserve its prerogatives from usurpation" (*ibid.*). The Abbé had never said anything of the sort: he had even underlined that it was impossible to establish any social precedence among the Shudras, who represented the overwhelming majority of the population. The same had been repeated over and over again throughout the 19th century.

theory concerned castes in general, he focused on the Brahmins, "the most faithful specimens of the Aryan type"; in his opinion, they alone had preserved "the purity of the superior race" (*ibid.*: 58).

The footnote on anthropometry found in *Remarques sur le regime des castes* (1900) was replaced in 1908 by a different one, introduced in Part III of the *Essays*. Crooke's data was finally exposed here:

> *When we look at his famous table of nasal indices, we are astonished to find that the Kayasths who, according to Brahmanic theory, are of Sudra race, have a higher place than the Brahmans, and yet more astonished to see the impure Chandalas ranking above the Rajbansis of royal blood. Examination of individual measurements raises more surprises. They show that a number of Brahmans tend (...) towards a negroid profile* (1971: 105).

It would seem impossible to disregard such facts, but this was exactly what Bouglé did, taking back the argument of Risley's exaggeration: "if anthropometry has exaggerated the value of its measurements, we must not, in another direction, exaggerate the value of our criticisms" (*ibid.*: 106).

The results revealed by Crooke and other authors only showed that "ethnic types have not stayed sufficiently clearly separated to enable us today to establish their differences objectively and evaluate them mathematically" (*ibid.*). Caste hierarchy was taken for granted, the demonstration of its existence being superfluous. The perverse effect of this passage must be noted. Risley's defence implied, after all, the implicit recognition of a failure: the impossibility of mathematically evaluating physical differences was tantamount to declaring the unsuccess of anthropometry itself.

But Bouglé's work, in its final form, already took into account the research led by Risley as Census Commissioner for 1901: the hierarchical arrangement of castes was now supposed to be directly obtained through Hindu public opinion. This perspective was also accepted by Bouglé. The way it was incorporated into the *Essays* accentuated, as we will see, the contradictory nature of the work.

IV

Deprived of social cohesion, India resisted unification. The country had known great empires but they had vanished without a trace (*ibid*.: 54). The British administration was the historical opportunity to endow the country with a principle of cohesion (*ibid*.: 82). But so far, the results had been scant. Indian civilization was divided, dismembered and on the verge of disintegration; how had it survived throughout its history?

Bouglé turned towards the Brahmins. His perspectives on the social function of the priests and, more generally, on religion were inevitably in line with those running throughout the *Essays*. Religion was primarily an obstacle to progress: "under a system that gives a religious tinge to every act in life and in particular to professional acts, every innovation appears as some fatal sin against thc ancestors. Even if one may feel the need one does not feel the right to innovate". Religion had contributed to "social anchylosis" (*ibid*.: 165).

Common Western conceptions credited the Hindu priests with "interested calculations" leading to the creation of castes. Bouglé's opinions were mere variations on this theme. The collective tendencies of the current social system reflected, he argued, ancient religious practices. It was "the habit of the close cult of the first familial groups that prevented castes from mingling" (*ibid*.: 60).

But the author also evoked the "force of attraction" exerted by the Brahmins on other castes. They had created "the masterly architecture which ranges the multiplicity of Hindu castes in a sacred order" (*ibid.*: 51). Instead of the usual insistence on the threat of disintegration, order – *order*, indeed – and a "masterly [social] architecture" were now evoked. Religion was, in short, a cause of both social division and integration.

Contradictory assertions marked the references to the Brahmins. Their ascendancy over the people was believed to be so unquestionable that "without arms or wealth, with but a lifted finger [they move or halt] things and men" (*ibid.* 160); as "a kind of man-god", imposing a "respect never enjoyed by the best armed tyrant", the priest displayed an absolute authority against which no 'philanthropic' voice could be heard (*ibid.*: 140). He held the population hypnotized (*ibid.*: 66). In another passage, however, one reads that "the masses were not so 'hypnotized' as has been said" (*ibid.*: 180). On the one hand, the priest's despotism was denounced; on the other, "tolerance, suppleness and plasticity" were the secret of his power (*ibid.*: 134).

The Brahmins *did not form* a "duly organized body"; their *varna*, comprising a large number of different *jatis*, was an example of disunity: they "lacked unity as much as the others" (*ibid.*: 54). Even so, they were described as "the only organized force which emerges in the universal divisiveness" of castes (*ibid.*: 127), "a centre for *the divided society*" (*ibid.*: 140, italics added). Embodying the ideal of Aryan purity and playing the role of sacrificers (*ibid.*: 59), their spiritual order was the "source of all social power" (ibid.: 160).

Had a principle of social cohesion finally been found? Had Bouglé managed to harmonize the first tendency of his "integral definition" – repulsion – with the priest's "force of attraction"? The answer is clear: he had not. As a matter of fact, *he could not.* The introduction of an aggregative force would destroy the main pillar of his thesis: castes "repel each other rather than attract". If the Brahmins' prestige was characterized as "the magnetic centre" of the social system (*ibid.*: 88), if they were supposed to *attract* castes as a magnet attracts iron chips, castes for their part could be compared to particles stubbornly *resisting attraction.* Bouglé claimed that the spirit of isolation that animated them resembled "an electrical charge in elder-pith balls [forcing] them to repel each other at the very moment of contact" (*ibid.*: 169).

A dead end is before us. We are told, on the one hand, that the Brahmin's attractive force "is powerful enough to take the place of the most efficient mechanisms" (*ibid.*: 130); but it is asserted, on the other, that this force is unable to abolish the aversion prevailing among castes. What should we think of an attractive force whose effects are neutralized by the dominant social impulse, determining divisiveness and antagonism? According to the author, "the sole, intimate, ever-present authority that regulates every detail of Hindu life, is precisely that which keeps the Hindus apart from each other" (*ibid.*: 65).

It is therefore not easy to grasp the nature of the role attributed to Brahmins as guarantors of some form of social cohesion. Consider the following statement: "If the individual groups, each isolated in its pride, tend to repel each other continually, they are none the less attracted, each one, towards a single summit" (*ibid.*: 89-90). As previously asserted, "a common respect for the Brahman orients [the castes] in the *same direction* and *weighs upon all their customs*" (*ibid.*: 51, italics added).

The two-facedness of Bouglé's discourse is particularly clear here. In order to emphasize *diversity* and *divisiveness*, it is argued that "a Hindu knows nothing of the customs of castes other than his own" (*ibid.*: 141); to stress *attraction*, a symmetrical view is sustained: all groups are exposed to a uniform influence. To properly establish the first principle of his "integral definition" – *repulsion* – the author declared the persistence of the rule keeping "the Hindus apart from each other"; to explain why, after all, fragmentation had not led to complete disintegration, he referred to the authority of priests, producing similar effects on the whole of society.

This again raised a problem. To the extent that the *same* influence was supposed to be exercised on all castes – thus sharing beliefs and customs – one should conclude that traits of resemblance, instead of insurmountable differences, had to be recognized.

***

Bouglé's twofold standpoint dominates his analysis of the hierarchy of castes. In a society where each group isolated itself and was indifferent to all others, the very conception of *caste precedence* is problematic. Who would care about relative positions? In fact, Bouglé noted, the Hindus "do not even have a public opinion to which they might appeal and so settle questions of precedence" (*ibid.*: 87).

However, another point of view, incompatible with the previous one, was introduced. As "certain traditional practices proclaim (…), there are superior castes universally revered or envied, and inferior castes, universally despised" (*ibid.*: 87-8). This contradicted the conception according to which each group remained ignorant of the others. Bouglé declared that "at least within the same province it is possible to derive a sort of official scale of caste dignity from public opinion" (*ibid.* 88). To know this official scale, the Brahmins should be consulted: their criteria regarding the castes from whom they accepted or refused cooked food "always decide precedence" (*ibid.*). The author was now inspired by Risley's latest view on social precedence "as conceived by Hindu public opinion". Like Risley, he believed that it was possible to obtain from the Brahmins a coherent picture of the status scale. This ultimately proved "the power with which the classical traditions of Brahmanism are imposed on public opinion" (*ibid.*). Let us admit for a moment that classical traditions had been *converted by Brahmins into general* opinion. But, in that case, why was it necessary to consult them for an accurate description of social precedence?

Bouglé's two points of view on hierarchy reflect the irresolvable conflict of the *Essays*. Public opinion was declared non-existent to emphasize the chaotic nature of caste hierarchy; it was acknowledged in order to highlight the priests' coordinating role:

Bouglé 1971: 87	**Bouglé 1971: 88**
[Hindus] "do not even have a public opinion to which they might appeal and so settle the question of precedence".	[Brahmins'] "criteria (…) always decide precedence; their operation (…) is proof of the power with which the classical traditions of Brahmanism are imposed on public opinion".
Caste society is a fragmented reality, made up of antagonistic elements.	Caste society is ordered by Brahmin's perspective.

Table 18 : *Bouglé on public opinion.*

Providing a counterweight to the disruptive tendency of the caste system, the Brahmins' power of attraction lent a semblance of sociological coherence to Bouglé's perspective. It is clear, however, that the main pillar of the *Essays*' construction was not the canon of sociology but the ideology of Western egalitarianism.

CHAPTER-8
AN UNFATHOMABLE IDEA

I

Ambiguity marked the reception of Risley's writings. His methods were not convincing but his conclusions seemed unassailable: the idea of caste hierarchy had been taken as proven.

Although most of Risley's superintendents said they were unable to recognize a principle of precedence among the people – *no social gradation whatsoever could be established*, Ananda Row had written – Shridhar Venkatesh Ketkar referred unhesitatingly to a caste *hierarchy*. In his opinion, a so-called "intermediate zone" – delimited by Brahmins and Untouchables – was occupied by "castes of innumerable gradations" (1909: 17) composing a hierarchy.

The reports of the latest census operations were among Ketkar's sources. But he did not trust the respective tables of precedence. The knowledge of the Pundits – to whom the British often turned for clarification – proved useless. The Pundits depended on "the authority of old books" which in no way reflected current social conditions (*ibid.*: 21). It was the responsibility of each group, the author stressed, to decide on the rules of conduct of its members and on their relations with other castes: "Consequently, whatever opinion the colleges of the Pundits may give, the actual precedence depends on what a caste can exact" (*ibid.*: 22).

Social precedence was, in his opinion, an irrelevant concept: "What does the precedence amount to?" – he asked. It simply referred to a vague public opinion according to which "one caste is better than another" (*ibid.*). *Public opinion* being an imprecise notion and *caste precedence* meaning "very little tangible good" (*ibid.*), how could Ketkar peremptorily proclaim the hierarchical character of Indian society (1909: 17)?

The ethnographic research which was associated with the census operations of 1901 had contradictory effects, its results having been interpreted in different ways. Risley's views – sometimes taken to be a good synthesis of the superintendents' opinions – were dominant. But the comparison of his perspectives with those extracted from the provincial reports could not fail to raise important questions.

***

In *The Religion of India,* Max Weber started by accepting Risley's idea that caste "is and remains essentially social rank", the rank of each group being "determined by the nature of its positive or negative relation to the Brahman" (1958 [1916]: 30). Although castes were alphabetically arranged in the report of 1903, the German sociologist roughly transcribed the list of criteria that Risley had prepared to guide his superintendents in their search for social precedence (see Chapter 6, Table 13). A simple work tool, this list presupposed a hierarchical tendency which, the Census Commissioner had assumed, would sooner or later become explicit. But this never happened.

Such was, however, the "order" to which Weber alluded in the section entitled *The Social Rank Order of the Castes in General* (*ibid.*: 44). The procedure was equivocal also because sets of castes, not particular groups, had been tentatively organized.

Weber seemed to believe that these sets were hierarchically arranged and that each of them included "further gradations of caste rank" (*ibid.*: 45). Yet he did not fail to acknowledge that these gradations presented "extremely varied characteristics" which made it difficult to design a coherent disposition. Social relationships appeared to be endowed with such complexity that, he ended up admitting, "it is perhaps impossible to determine the rank order of castes" (*ibid.*: 47). He thus stated, on the one hand, that the *rank order* of castes was the goal towards which the Hindu social system was oriented; and, on the other, that this order seemed indecipherable:

"A profound estrangement usually exists between the castes, and often deadly jealousy and hostility as well, precisely because the castes are completely oriented towards social rank" (*ibid.*: 38).	"It is perhaps impossible to determine the rank order of the castes; it is contested and subject to change" (*ibid.*: 47).

Weber's scepticism about a possible order of social precedence did not prevent him from delving, later in the book, into the problem of its origin. In this regard, economic factors, along with racial arguments, should not be ruled out. But Risley's anthropometric approach was not convincing: "one should not assume that the caste order could be explained as a product of 'race psychology' – by mysterious tendencies inherent in the 'blood' or the 'Indian soul'" (*ibid.*: 124).

The order of caste precedence was thus proclaimed regardless of

- the unaccepted explanation of its origin; and

- the fact that the order itself was "perhaps impossible to determine".

***

By the beginning of the 20th century, many authors acknowledged that the hypothesis concerning caste hierarchy was not clearly corroborated by the facts. "At the time of the census of 1901", W. H. Thompson wrote, "an attempt was made in dealing with the statistics of castes to set each down in order according to its place in Hindu society, but it was found by no means easy to do so". The difficulty continued to be attributed to the absence of a common point of view on social precedence: "there is no general consensus of opinion on some points" (1923: 345). As before, castes were presented in the alphabetical order of their names.

According to J. T. Marten, the Hindu population saw in the census operations an opportunity "to press for recognition of social claims and to secure, if possible, a step upwards in the social ladder" (1924: 223). Such a social ladder, however, was impossible to describe. No satisfactory classification had been found: the only solution was, again, an alphabetical arrangement. What the author said he had before his eyes was nothing more than "a rough order of social precedence" (*ibid.*: 224), made up of elements he did not even know how to name. Given its "enormous complexity" and the impossibility of properly sorting out most of the population, he could only consider three large divisions: Brahmins at the top; "depressed classes" at the bottom; and in the "middle" a zone of... "non-Brahmin castes" (*ibid.*: 224-25).

The profusion and diversity of castes were often evoked to justify the difficulty of talking about it. In the words of N. K. Dutt, "the system is such a peculiar and complex thing that no satisfactory definition is possible" (1931: 1). Admitting that "there is some hierarchical gradation among the castes", he merely observed that "the most recognised position [was] that of the Brahmans at the top" (*ibid.:* 3), leaving his readers the freedom to imagine how, from top to bottom, the succession of groups was arranged.

O'Malley referred likewise to "a graduated scale culminating in the Brahman and descending to what are known as the Untouchables or depressed classes". The principles of the system remained elusive. Between Brahmins and Untouchables there was "no detailed warrant of precedence in which each individual caste has an assigned place, but rather a social stratification in which castes are grouped in different layers" (1932: 11).

Stressing the "splendid work" Risley had achieved (1932: 101), Ghurye noted however that the method adopted did not satisfactorily clarify the whole caste issue. The conflict between Risley's theoretical conjectures and the observed reality was implicitly expressed as follows:

"Everywhere in India there is a definite scheme of social precedence amongst the castes" (Ghurye 1932: 6)	"The order of social precedence amongst the individual castes of any class cannot be made definite, because not only is there no ungrudging acceptance of such rank but also the ideas of the people on this point are very nebulous and uncertain" (*ibid.*)

Hutton was even more assertive. Sceptical about the tables of precedence elaborated during the census operations of 1901, he made it clear that the results obtained differed from those Risley claimed to be proud of: "he [had] failed", Hutton concluded peremptorily (1933: 433). In spite of this, the idea of caste hierarchy gradually became unquestionable, as if it was inherent in the natural order of things.

How did systematic ethnographic research deal with the problem? In this respect, M. Srinivas' work deserves special attention.

II

Srinivas distinguished two forms of social structure in India. He questioned the "popular idea of caste as a rigid five-fold hierarchy" (four *varnas* plus "mixed classes"), emphasizing the existence of "innumerable groups" that did not obey inflexible constraints (1952: 219-20). A *rigid* hierarchical model should even be abandoned: "The fivefold system does not do justice to the complexity of the caste system as it exists" (*ibid.*: 220).

Society *as it exists* implied friction and divergence as Srinivas noted in several passages of his monograph on the Coorgs. This can be partly explained by the coexistence of very different groups, each of them endowed with "a certain amount of cultural and ritual autonomy"; consequently, "any attempt to fit them into a hierarchy results in disputes as to relative status" (*ibid.*).

Although the author stressed that the facts hardly fit a *rigid* model, he could not do without the notion of hierarchy – it was "present everywhere", in his words. What model did he have in mind? Would it be possible to substitute a *rigid* by a *flexible* hierarchy? Srinivas seems to have admitted a sort of "tolerant" hierarchy, indifferent to disagreement or antagonism. An example of this was given when he noted that the integration of a non-Hindu group into the caste system is only fully achieved once it becomes a caste in itself: "The exact position which such a group occupies in the hierarchy might be a matter of dispute, *but that is not important*" (*ibid.*: 219, italics added). Differences of opinion are frequent: "disputes as to relative status are a feature specially of castes of the middle region" (*ibid.*: 220) – an "essential feature", it was even pointed out (*ibid.*: 25). This is a surprising statement. Consensus had generally been considered a *sine qua non* of social precedence but, from the point of view now proclaimed, it was not required.

It goes without saying that "tolerance" for divergences regarding relative status abolishes the idea of hierarchy. A subtle and ductile hierarchy is indeed a contradiction in terms: actually, Srinivas could not abandon the idea of a "rigid" hierarchy – that is to say, the idea of hierarchy *tout court*. Let us see how he managed to adjust reality to his description of caste hierarchy.

***

Srinivas repeatedly emphasized that disputes over relative status occur in the "middle region" of the structure (*ibid*.: 220), while the social condition of the groups placed at the "extremes" would be well defined: "It is possible everywhere to say who are the Brahmins and Untouchables, but there is great confusion in the middle regions" (*ibid*.: 25). The "great confusion" attributed to the "middle" zone was certainly not an argument in favour of hierarchy. But Srinivas admitted that instability is also observed at both ends of the structure: "In Mysore, Untouchables do not accept food and water from smiths, and from Mārka Brahmins. They believe such acceptance would defile them" (*ibid*.: 28). And in another passage: "The Brahmins and Untouchables are known to belong to either extreme, though (…) the presence of some subdivisions of Brahmins who are said to be inferior to practically every other caste complicates matters" (*ibid*.: 220). Why does the presence of low-status Brahmins *complicate matters*? The answer is clear: it does not fit the hierarchical model. In other words, Srinivas only expected to find Brahmins in fixed positions previously determined according to *indisputable hierarchical rules*.

The author returned to this topic in later works: "While uncertainty as to mutual rank is a marked characteristic of the middle regions of the *jati* system, it is not restricted to them" (1976: 170). The place of the Brahmins had to be reconsidered: "Even the popular idea that the Brahmins occupy the top position in the hierarchy needs to be modified". They do not form a homogeneous group "but a congeries of similar-yet-different *jatis*" (*ibid.*). The fact had long been recognized, but the earlier formula according to which "it is possible everywhere to say who are the Brahmins and Untouchables" testifies to the belief in the strength of a conception which Srinivas himself thought should be abandoned.

***

The dilemma contained within the discussion about hierarchy appeared most clearly in a 1955 article, *The Social System of a Mysore Village*. Table 19 summarizes Srinivas' description of the castes of Rampura:

Rank Group	Caste		
I	*(A) Hoysala Karnāmaka* Brahman *(B)Mādhva*	*Lingāyat*	*Smith*
II	Peasant – Shepherd – Trader – Oilman – Potter – (A) Fisherman – Washerman – Barber – Basketmaker – Toddyman (B) Swineherd		
III	Untouchable		

Table 19: *Hierarchical list of castes in Rampura* (ibid. 1955: 23).

Srinivas did not, in any way, conceal the difficulties he faced in his field research. In his opinion, however, such obstacles should not dissuade him from engaging in a graphic representation of the scale of social status – "for the existence of a hierarchy and the preoccupation of village people with it are beyond doubt" (*ibid.*: 22). But it is the very possibility of such an exercise that Srinivas' considerations invite us to question: "it is difficult, if not impossible, to determine the exact, or even the approximate, place of each caste in the hierarchical system" (*ibid.*: 19-20); "any attempt to arrange the castes of a village or local area into a hierarchy is (…) both difficult and fraught with risk"; "any hierarchical list is necessarily tentative and arguable" (*ibid.*: 22).

A hierarchical list like the one presented above could hardly account for what had been considered an "essential feature" of the system: disagreement and dispute over relative positions. Although Srinivas had stated that it was practically impossible to know the exact – or even approximate – place of each caste, he made it clear that he could not dismissed the rigid hierarchical model. An implicit reliance on more or less *fixed positions* is inevitably assumed in the process of building a hierarchical list. It was as a result of this tacit reliance that elements whose status seemed excessively ambiguous were placed outside the structure. An example was provided by Smiths, whose status was considered inferior to that of individuals in most castes, including the Holeya Untouchables. Smiths, however, declared that they only accepted cooked food from Brahmins. Given their "strange position", Srinivas placed them (along with Lingayats) in a separate column of his list. To what extent, then, could different perspectives of different castes be accepted? How could one recognize the threshold beyond which certain forms of *difference* became intolerable?

Such difficulties led Srinivas to admit the imperfection of his list. Some castes "may be put approximately into a hierarchy as is shown in [Table 19] but I am convinced that such a ladder-like arrangement is not a perfect way of representing the situation" (*ibid.*: 24).

By acknowledging the "great confusion" of the "middle" region of the structure and holding that consensus was not required, that divergence and dispute were an "essential feature" of the system, and that, for this very reason, "a ladder-like arrangement [was] not a perfect way of representing" the caste universe, Srinivas attributed to hierarchy a specificity which in no way agreed with the dominant conception.

***

Regarding inter-caste relationships, different arguments are put forward to justify a claim to singularity: purity, diet, occupation, a particular caste custom, a significant event recorded by a mythical narrative... But the reasons given by a particular caste to support its demands are not necessarily accepted or approved by the others.

This is a privileged arena for disputes – the "essential feature" of the system that Srinivas, nevertheless, sought to suppress. To eliminate conflict between the different perspectives, he considered two possibilities: either accepting the point of view of a particular group or building a hierarchy according to his own criteria. Although the Holeya Untouchable declared himself superior to the Smith, Srinivas noted that several impediments were imposed on him. He was required to live away from the central area of the village; he did not have access to the temples of the upper castes, etc. The Smith "has, or had, certain other disabilities". It was, then, necessary to compare the respective situations in order to determine which of the two castes enjoyed a higher status. The analyst could not aspire to full objectivity because his construction involved the "evaluation of statements made by his informants". But he alone would be able to assess, compare and order sociological specificities: his opinion would be "less subjective than the claims of any one of the castes themselves" (*ibid.*: 25).

In other words, divergences and disputes rested on biased considerations which should be reappraised. Srinivas had to weigh up the different claims in order to choose... the most consistent one. How did he define such consistency? To begin with, is it possible to compare the criteria put forward by the different castes? Is a vegetarian diet comparable to a mythical story? What is the sociological merit of this method of comparison?

The need to rank the groups according to a framework of more or less *fixed positions* overshadows the fact that sociological specificities are often incommensurable: every context triggers an adequate response expressing a particular facet of the group's identity. This is understated by Srinivas' assertion that disputes over relative status "are not important". The spirit of hierarchy that animated his whole project prevented him from recognizing that such disputes *are* indeed sociologically relevant as main pieces of the play involving mirrored identities. The elements of this play compose a symbolic structure that is incompatible with hierarchical requirements.

III

Emphasizing the ambiguity of ritual status and the absence of a "fixed" hierarchy, H. N. C. Stevenson posed the following question: "how do people know which groups are of high and which of low ritual status, or where the line of untouchability must be drawn"? In his opinion, the *pollution concept* provided the answer (1954: 49). The problem persisted, however. According to Srinivas, pollution is conveyed "by contact with lower castes" (1955: 20). But doubts from the past continued to be embarrassing. Eighty years earlier, Cornish had observed that Europeans could not determine what a "high" or a "low" caste really was; "[why is it that] some *low* castes are *low*?", Yalman would later ask (1960: 102).

It was well known that certain castes with a "low" status refuse the cooked food of "higher" ones. And it is not uncommon for individuals with a "low" status to be assigned important ritual functions. Such facts had been reported for a long time but had not attracted the attention they deserved. In 1872, Hunter noted that, when pilgrims approached the entrance of the great temple of Jagannatha in Puri (Orissa), a man of the sweeper caste stroked them with his broom to purify them of their sins"; they then had to promise, "on pain of losing all the benefits of pilgrimage, not to disclose the events of the journey or the secrets of the shrine" (1872: 142).

The interpretation of such data has been inhibited by hierarchical assumptions and commonly accepted perspectives: "A polluting person is always in the wrong", Mary Douglas proclaimed in a classic study on the concepts of *pollution* and *taboo*; "he has developed some wrong condition or simply crossed some line which should not have been crossed and this displacement unleashes danger for someone" (1966: 113). This was generally accepted by Wendy Doniger. The ascetic, as he emerges in the Mahabharata, challenges the orthodox perspective according to which everyone must remain faithful, throughout life, to the values of the group into which he was born: "In terms of Mary Douglas's paradigm, the rising ascetic becomes 'dirt'; that is, he is out of place, out of order" (1980: 66).

"Dirt offends against order", according to Mary Douglas (1966: 2): *pollution* and *order* are considered to be incompatible. This is questionable. The connection between "dirt" and "impurity", on the one hand, and the idea of the "creative power" of pollution, on the other, are often affirmed by mythical thought, as recognized by Doniger herself. According to some versions, "Pārvatī produced Skanda from her own spittle, and Gaṇeśa was born from the water in which she washed herself after she had made love with Śiva

(...), or from the rubbings of her body when she anointed herself in the bath" (1980: 37).

This view is corroborated by countless examples and deserves further investigation. A Coorgh myth – a version of which was included by Srinivas in his 1952 monograph – had been published in 1899 by Emma Rauschenbusch-Clough. It must be reproduced here:

> *In ancient times there lived in the Malabar country six brothers and a sister. They went together to Coorg, but the brothers were not pleased because the sister came with them, and they decided to spoil her caste. On the way they were hungry, and said to the sister: "Prepare us some food". She replied, "There is neither fire nor rice." They said: "We will give you rice, but you must boil it without fire." She replied: "I will boil it without fire, but you must eat it without salt." To this the brothers agreed.*
>
> *The sister saw a cow and milked her, letting the milk fall into the vessel of rice. Then she went to the bank of a river, buried the pot in the sand, and it began to boil. The brothers awoke from their sleep and ate.*
>
> *Later, while sitting together, chewing betel, they said, "Let us see whose betel is the reddest." They all spat out the betel into their hands, looked at it, and the brothers threw it behind their heads. The sister, deluded by this, threw the betel back into her mouth and went on chewing. The brothers now said she had lost her caste. She was excessively grieved and wept bitterly.*
>
> *One of the brothers threw an arrow, and ordered his sister to go with it and stay where it fell. She assumed the form of a crane and alighted on a Pariah, working in the rice fields. He became possessed with a devil*

> *and ran towards the mango tree, where the arrow was sticking. A temple was built around this tree, where the Coorgs still worship the sister of the six brothers, especially at her annual feast* (1899: 59-61).

Srinivas' version was shorter, ending with the chewing of the betel leaves, the only episode he wanted to retain. It allowed him to affirm that "faeces, urine, semen, menstrual blood, spittle, and parings of nail and hair are all ritually impure" (1952: 105-06). Having reintroduced the chewed stuff into her mouth, the sister became impure, lost her caste and was condemned by her brothers to become the goddess of the Untouchable Poleyas.

Mary Douglas referred to Srinivas' version to illustrate her own conceptions. But her perspective on the caste system was quite different to that of Srinivas. He maintained that the hierarchy of castes did not involve a linear arrangement or fixed positions. And, in certain passages of his work, he saw the lack of agreement and disputes over relative status as an essential aspect of the system. Mary Douglas asserted, however, that each group "in a local region is conscious of its relative standing in the scale of purity" (1966: 123). In her opinion, the Coorg social system represented "a body in which by the division of labour the head does the thinking and praying and the most despised parts carry away waste matter" (*ibid.*). This was, at most, an example of a Western way of thinking about the caste system. But the Indian "scale of purity" evoked by Mary Douglas is an abstraction. Her conception of a social structure in which the purest castes *think and pray* while the most impure ones *remove the waste matter* is more than a simplification: it obscures the Coorg myth she wanted to interpret.

In both versions, the girl associated – in different ways – with the Untouchables is, from the start, the most gifted partner, only excluded by cunning and perfidy. In this respect, Rauschenbusch-Clough's version is particularly revealing. The incident that converted the sister into a polluting character was a qualifying test. Her condemnation and affinity with untouchability highlighted her spiritual superiority: the arrow shot by one of the brothers marked the precise place where a temple was to be built and where she would be worshipped by the Coorgs. It was with the help of an Untouchable – on whom she alighted in the form of a crane – that a sacred place could be reached.

***

In this regard, other aspects of Srinivas' ethnographic research should be mentioned. The Coorgs, self-proclaimed Kshatriyas,[1] usually summoned a low-caste Banna to perform their ancestor-propitiation ceremonies. The fact that he was "the master of the complicated technique of ancestor-propitiation, and that he [was] possessed by these spirits during the propitiation, temporarily put him in a high position", Srinivas noted (1952: 43). He saw here a mark of disharmony between *ritual* and *secular* contexts, an "inconsistency" of which new examples could be found. A Brahmin could certainly be recognized as "master of a highly complicated ritual technique" – and this would be considered "normal". But let us assume along with Srinivas that such a function is fulfilled by a poor Brahmin who is economically dependent on a wealthy Shudra. This was described as atypical, and the author concluded: "Where the Brahmin priest is also a scholar or holy man there does not seem to be any inconsistency between his ritual and secular roles" (*ibid.*). The notion of "inconsistency" shows once again that Srinivas' implicit model consisted of a system with fixed positions, corresponding to unambiguous social statuses.

The distinction between ritual and secular contexts is itself arguable. Let us consider the relationship between a Coorg and a

1. Their wealth, their power and their "martial look" seemed to justify such a claim. Their diet, however, included liquor and pork, causing scornful comments by members of other castes.

Madivala or Washerman. Although the latter was a man with a very low status, he was chosen to be the ritual purifier of a Coorg house whenever a birth or death occurred (*ibid.*: 41). This, Srinivas stressed, "is not *consistent* with the position he normally occupies in the caste hierarchy" (*ibid.*: 85, italics added). Such *inconsistency*, he assumed, tended to disappear since, "nowadays (…), Coorgs increasingly call on a Brahmin to purify the house on the twelfth day [after the birth of a child]" (*ibid.*).

In these examples, "inconsistent" situations reflect what is considered to be one of the fragilities of the social fabric, a disharmony to be banished. But why is it considered incongruent that a ritual activity can be performed by a Banna at the request of a high-caste man? The reason is obvious: in a hierarchical framework such a situation is unthinkable. Likewise, the Washerman's purifying role is conceived as a sociological implausibility – only to be repaired when a Brahmin claims that function as his own privilege.

The replacement of the ritual services of a Washerman with those of a Brahmin was seen by Srinivas as "part of the general process of Sanskritization[2] of Coorg customs" (*ibid.*). But even if Sanskritization could account for the Coorg's strategy of raising the prestige of their caste, it would not explain the substitution of a low-status ritualist for a higher-status ritualist, since each time a Brahmin accepted to replace a Madivala, the logic underlying caste hierarchy had to be questioned.

The Madivala deserves attention for another reason. Also in his case, a hiatus was postulated between two forms of activity, the first corresponding to the position the Washerman "normally occupies" in the hierarchy (*secular* role), the second concerning his competence as a purifier (*ritual role*). This discontinuity is

2. Sanskritization itself partly testifies to hierarchical assumptions. See Konale and Bhat.

unacceptable, as Srinivas implicitly recognized: "It is probable the washerman was employed as purifier because of his occupation" (*ibid.*: 85). In the author's words, the clothes washed by the Madivala "are not only clean but ritually pure (*madi*)" (*ibid.:* 40-41). In short, *ritual* purity was achieved through the "secular" role of an "impure" agent. At no time does the Madivala cease to fulfil a "secular" function to assume a "ritual" one; he did not abandon one aspect of his identity to adopt a new one. Access to the most sacred places of a Coorg house (the kitchen and the central hall) was forbidden to him; and if "he has to enter them in the exercise of his duties (...) they are purified subsequently" (*ibid.*: 85). There is no boundary between the different moments of his intervention: they are entangled aspects of the same process.

IV

A monograph by S. C. Dube, published in 1955, was focused on Shamirpet, a village of the Telugu-speaking part of Hyderabad. The author presented what he also considered to be a social hierarchy based on the conception of pollution. "Twice-Born" castes at the top and Untouchables at the bottom defined once again the space assigned to a "middle zone", occupied by different "Occupational castes":

"Twice-Born" Castes
Brahmin (Priests)
Komti (Traders)

Occupational castes:
Kapu-Reddi (Agriculturists) *Kummari* (Poters) *Golla* (Shepherds)
Kapu-Muttarasi (Agriculturists)
Sale (Weavers) *Gaondla* (Toddy-tappers)
Sakali (Washermen) *Mangali* (Barbers)

Vaddar (Stone-workers) *Erkala* (Hunters and Mat-makers) *Pichha-Kuntla* (Minstrels) Untouchable castes: *Mala* *Madiga*

Table 20: *Castes of Shamirpet* (Dube 1955: 36).

Like Srinivas, Dube excluded from his overall framework some castes (Carpenters, Blacksmiths and Goldsmiths) whose social status was considered to be "rather uncertain"[3] – "neither very high nor very low" (*ibid.*: 38). For unspecified reasons, they could have been placed below the Kapu-Reddis, the Kummaris and the Gollas but – again for unclear reasons – it could not "be said that they rank equal to or below the Sale - Gaondla group" (*ibid.*). They were "unclassifiable".

The Brahmins were followed by the Komtis, who were followed in turn by three groups (Kapu-Reddis, Kummaris, Gollas) whose relations seemed established on a basis of equality. One might have expected that they would adopt similar forms of behaviour in their relations with other castes. But this was not the case. Kapu-Reddis and Gollas accepted the food of Kapu-Muttarasis, who, for this reason, might be considered to be their equals. But the Kummaris refused their food, a fact which, of course, raised difficulties.

Two Untouchable groups, Malas and Madigas, were also presented hierarchically, the former refusing the cooked food of

3. Carpenters, Blacksmiths, Goldsmiths, Carvers of figures in wood or stone and Workers in bell-metal make up the Panch Bramha group. Brought together by alliance and commensality, they "constitute a distinct group of their own" (*ibid.*: 37). Only the first three of these castes were represented in Shamirpet.

the latter. The Dakkals, defined as the lower section of the Madigas, were distinguished by their refusal of food from the hands of any non-Madiga person:

> *The Brahmin, who is at the apex of the caste-hierarchy, refuses to partake of food at the hands of anyone with a social status lower than his own (...). And it is a juxtaposition that the lowest of the low castes refuses food from all communities of the higher levels, including the Brahmins* (ibid.: 42).

Dube did not dwell on the meaning of that "juxtaposition". But it is not enough to say that the ethnographic facts do not fit the hierarchical model; they are often distorted by the simple attempt to make them compatible with it.

When Dube published his book on Shamirpet, there was considerable information on the "unexpected" nature of social relations in this context. The Komtis (Komatis), placed by the author "at the top" of the social structure of Shamirpet, immediately after the Brahmins, maintained powerful symbolic relations with the Madigas. "It would not occur to any one", Rauschenbusch-Clough had written, "that there could be a connection between the wealthy, prosperous Komati and the poor, despised Madiga if peculiar customs did not exist that point to some kind of tie between them. The Komatis are not pleased with a reference to these customs" (1899: 46).

Each time a marriage was concluded among the Komatis, the presence of the Madigas was required: "Though the Madiga would not be a guest in any way desirable, he must be invited, lest ill-fortune befall the young couple". The Madigas themselves showed no signs that they were happy with such an invitation, apparently considering it insulting: "should a Komati dare to extend it openly, his messenger might be treated roughly at the hands of the irate Madigas". According to Rauschenbusch-Clough, even "the light with which the fire is kindled during the marriage ceremony must come from the house of the Madiga" (*ibid.*: 47; also see Thurston 1909, vol. III; Elmore 1915).

Dube did not ignore the role played by the Madigas in the annual festival dedicated to the village goddess of smallpox. It was up to a group of drum-beaters of this caste to announce the ceremony throughout the lanes of Shamirpet; they also started the celebrations the following day, heading the procession that should proceed from the centre of Shamirpet to the goddess's shrine: "[They] walk at the head of the procession, followed at some distance by the Deshmukh [the village headman] and other respectable people and village elders, and then by the common people of the village" (1955: 112).

But this does not do justice to the importance of the Madigas' traditional function. In Thurston's words, an unmarried Madiga woman (the Matangi, a favourite deity of which she is supposed to be the incarnation) "[presides] at the purificatory ceremonies that precede all festivities". Her ability to exercise this function is justified by "prophetic utterances, and her nomination is not confirmed till she has obtained divine approval" (1909, IV: 296). Still according to Thurston,

> *The master of the ceremonies, his male and female relations, then stand in a line, and the Mātangi runs round and round them, uttering what appear to be meaningless exclamations, spitting upon all of them, and touching them with her stick. Her touch and saliva are believed to purge all uncleanliness of body and soul, and are invited by men who would ordinarily scorn to approach her* (ibid.).

As Elmore deemed it necessary to emphasize, "not only the Madigas but the higher castes, even Brahmans, stand in line, as anxious to be spat upon and touched by her stick and her person as are the lowest" (1915: 31). Such facts were often declared unintelligible: "it passes one's comprehension how [the Mātangi] should be honoured with the task of purifying the soul and body of high class Reddis and purse-proud Kōmatis" (Thurston 1909, IV: 296-97). Nor is the role of "purifying through impurities" – to use Alf Hiltebeitel's expression (1980: 211) – consistent with common sense.

There are many examples of the "incomprehensible" power attributed to "low" status castes. Again in relation to the Komatis, the Madigas seem to enjoy (or to have enjoyed) important prerogatives. It has been mentioned that, in certain circumstances, they had the power to "put a stop to a marriage by coming to the house at which it is to be celebrated, chopping away the plantain trunks which decorate the marriage booth, and carrying them off". This suggests, according to Thurston, that the Komatis' right "to stand there is not recognised" (Thurston 1909, III: 327). They had taken ownership of lands formerly occupied by Madigas (and other now depressed castes), a fact probably explaining their deference towards them.

The hypothesis is far-fetched. Nevertheless, puzzling powers over the land are often imputed to different "low" status castes. That is the case of the Balahis of Central India, studied by Stephan Fuchs. Spinning and weaving had been their traditional occupations but the industrialization of textile production forced them to adopt new professional activities. Many of them became field-workers for landowners and cultivators. Fuchs was not impressed by the skills they revealed in their new activities, even when they took care of their own land: "the Balahi is indolent, ignorant and improvident. His heart is not in his work" (1950: 373-74); "[h]is fields are usually badly prepared for the sowing, he is often careless about the proper time for the sowing, he knows little about the selection of seeds and rotation of crops" (*ibid.*: 374). In spite of this, "high-caste farmers like to employ Balahi field-labourers for the sowing of their fields. They believe that the crops will grow well if Balahis do the sowing" (*ibid.*: 291). It was not the memory of old land rights that the current owners intended to recognize and respect: only the ambition to have a good harvest determines the owners of the land to request their intervention.

Referring to examples borrowed from Thurston and others, but leaving the beaten track, A. M. Hocart drew attention to the fact that "they lend a very different complexion to the Indian caste system from the orthodox – I might say, official – view". And he added:

> *The humblest have their privileges which they can enforce against their betters, and the highest have their disabilities. The system has been judged by the theory, and the theory is very different from the practice. The brahmans who put forth such arrogant claims in* The Laws of Manu *and other works were probably finding compensation for the fact that they were entirely in the hands of their inferiors* (1950: 64-5, note 5).

***

It is often claimed, Adrian Mayer acknowledged, that "those castes which are most exclusive eat from nobody else, and the lowest castes eat from nearly everyone (…). In practice, however, the hierarchy is not so simply composed" (1960: 34). The echo of Srinivas' considerations is found in some of his remarks on the subject:

> *Many writers have pointed out that the hierarchy is clear at the top and bottom, but has an imprecise form in its middle reaches. It is worth going further, and considering whether inter-caste relations are not even more different in these two instances, stemming from a real difference in outlook. Whereas castes in the*

> *lowest and highest ranks both think and say that they are higher than their neighbours, the castes in the middle may think they are higher, but say publicly that they are equal* (ibid.: 44).

Such observations could have led to the hierarchical model being questioned. But that did not happen. Mayer simply reiterated the terms noted by Srinivas: "In a hierarchy in which there are anomalies of rank, there is room for alteration, for a certain fluidity" (*ibid.*: 47).

V

The diversity of ethnographic methods proposed to achieve a hierarchical classification testify to the conjectural nature of the whole operation. Kathleen Gough pointed out that diet, rules concerning marriage and etiological myths among other elements helped define ritual rank but were "selectively and somewhat inconsistently employed". She therefore noted the difficulty of saying what would be the "real bases of the ritual rank" (1959: 115). Pauline Mahar submitted a questionnaire to a set of eighteen individuals from Khalapur, a village in Uttar Pradesh, to determine the "ritual distance" between them. Each of these individuals was required to declare whether, for example, he accepted physical contact with persons from another group in the same village; whether he tolerated their presence in the space reserved for the preparation of meals, etc. (1959: 129). Each respondent composed in this way an "individual hierarchy", a collective pattern that supposedly emerged from their answers. A perfectly consistent over-all ranking would require an impossible unanimity.

Stressing that a high degree of agreement among the people was necessary for the construction of a caste hierarchy, McKim Marriott referred to the context of two villages in Uttar Pradesh. Villagers were primarily invited to distribute the castes of the region into vaguely defined categories: "Highest"; "High"; "Low" and "Lowest" (1965 [1960]: 11). An alleged "strong consensus" among them was supposed to go further and follow the even more subtle distinctions of an even more extraordinary nomenclature: "High", "Very high"; "Merely high"; "Not so high"… (*ibid.*: 11-2).

Marriott admitted the limits of a "high degree of consensus" among villagers. Their unanimity did not go beyond placing castes "within the agreed major or minor blocks"; in fact, they did "not agree closely on the exact ranks to which single castes should be assigned" (*ibid.*: 12). The stratified social order reflected the nature of interactions between groups. The most important ones – the ritual interactions – involved transactions concerning certain kinds of food and services. They expressed a "ritual hierarchy", but this coexisted with non-ritual hierarchies of interaction, determined by economic and political considerations: "Thus the degree of consensus on caste rank (…) is affected ultimately by correlations among all hierarchies of interaction, both ritual and non-ritual" (*ibid.*: 19).

In *An Objective Method for Determining the Collective Caste Hierarchy of an Indian Village*, Stanley Freed noted first that in Shanti Nagar (a fictitious name for a village near Delhi), "agreement among villagers about the ranking of castes is close enough so that one can determine the approximate rank in the hierarchy of most castes" (1963: 879). But what he considered the villagers' perspective on the *approximate rank* in the local hierarchy was nothing more than a singularly indefinite assessment, castes being designated as "high", "medium" or "low". Like Marriott, Freed was forced to recognize that the villagers were not able to assign exact positions. Agreement, after all, was not obvious: "some villagers may assign each caste to a separate rank; some may say that two or more castes have equal rank; and some may assign relatively high rank to a caste which others rank relatively low". The author also stressed the coexistence of multiple criteria: "the villagers may use different criteria in constructing their rankings; or even if they use the same criteria, they may weigh them differently".

Freed thus assumed the coexistence of multiple forms of social distinction, admitting therefore different status scales within the same context. And although he started by affirming a relative consensus – "a close enough agreement" – concerning caste hierarchy, shortly afterwards he saw himself forced to turn back: "the *lack of agreement* among the villagers about caste ranking raised the question: what single hierarchy would best express the collective opinion of the villagers and how many discrete, significant ranks does it contain"? (1963: 879, italics added). Instead of suggesting a specific ranking criterion, he hoped that a hierarchical pattern would be spontaneously supplied by the respondents. A set of movable cards, each bearing the name of a caste, was presented to a limited number of villagers, who were asked to regroup them hierarchically. Once again, the results obtained – a "collective caste hierarchy", as Freed called it – were no more than the expression of "a statistical test of significance" (*ibid.*).

CHAPTER-9
HIERARCHY AND SELF REFERENCE

I

Self-reference is one of the main obstacles to the Western understanding of non-Western realities: we always start from ourselves (1975 [1964]: 10), observed Louis Dumont in *Indian Civilization and Us* [*La Civilisation Indienne et Nous*]. This inescapable difficulty, he added, can be dealt with either naively or consciously. The alternative is largely illusory, because the distinction is hard, if not impossible, to establish. Dumont believed, however, that the risks of subjectivity could be reduced: good practices recommend that the different aspects of the observed reality should be interrelated and subordinate to the whole. Even this, he admitted, was perhaps a "too optimistic view" (*ibid.*: 13, n. 1). The author agreed with Marcel Mauss who advocated the "inventory" of essential categories in present and past societies. Once duly recognized, *the* "difference between civilizations" would make it possible to situate the comparative approach at the level of the "reference categories themselves". Here again, the success of the approach seems doubtful. How can the relevant distinctions between civilizations be objectively identified?

The issue was discussed again in the "Preface" of the first edition of *Homo Hierarchicus*. Dumont asserted that the "embryonic state" of sociological studies on the caste system was due to the fact that "the main effort has not been directed towards the proper aim of questioning our preconceived ideas" (1980 [1966]: xlvii). An inaccurate idea of hierarchy was responsible for the "slow progress" in this field. The "true" meaning of the word had been inflected by special circumstances of "our" own history: the advent of modernity with its emphasis on equality. Currently, Western common sense mainly refers to *social stratification*, but "that is not hierarchy proper, nor the deepest root of what is so called" (*ibid.*: 19). One may wonder how a society supposedly obsessed by egalitarianism had refused the "real" hierarchy while preserving a surrogate in the form of "social stratification".

But the problem cannot be reduced to a mere distortion of meaning. Certain passages of *Homo Hierarchicus* asserted that the "old" notion had not been simply reshaped but converted into an object of denial, preserved "at the heart of the 'unthought'" (*ibid.*: xvi). Swept away from general consciousness, it had become *invisible*: "modern man is virtually incapable of fully recognizing it" (*ibid.*: xlvii). The process left such deep marks that "even sociologists and philosophers seem to speak of 'hierarchy' reluctantly and with averted eyes" (*ibid.*: 19).

Yet, strangely enough, the long-repressed phenomenon came abruptly to light. Something unexpected had occurred: *Homo Hierarchicus* testified to the resurgence of the ancient concept. But the more Dumont insisted on the unnoticeable character of the alleged old notion – transformed into a "kind of taboo", as later asserted – the more incomprehensible its re-emergence became.

After stating that modern man "fails to notice" hierarchy (*ibid.*: xlvii) [*il ne la voit point*], Dumont seemed to have changed his mind. The notion had not really disappeared: Western scholars simply attempted to get rid of it... without much success. It had subsisted, even forcing modern man to pay attention to it, though when confronted with its re-appearance, he tended "to eliminate it as an epiphenomenon". Refusal was therefore transmuted into acceptance: "Should he finally accept it, as I did [*c'était mon cas*], he must still take pains to see it as it really is, without attributing imaginary properties to it" (*ibid.*). One may, therefore, infer that the sociologist accepted "something" whose true nature was largely unknown; only subsequently did he mysteriously manage, not without effort, to understand what he was actually dealing with...

Under what circumstances could the "old" concept have attracted attention? Dumont simply asserted that "all the difficulties vanish if we keep it firmly before our eyes, accustom ourselves to following its outlines and implications" (*ibid.*). It had been enough *to look* carefully to make reappear that which, as initially affirmed, had remained in the shade for a very long time.

***

Before specifying how "true" hierarchy should be understood, Dumont found it useful to clarify his position in the field of the social sciences: "I owe everything, or almost everything, to the French tradition of sociology. For not only has it nurtured me, my ambition is to extend it" (*ibid.*: xlv-xlvi). He declared, in particular, his intellectual debt to Célestin Bouglé, whose *Essays* had been a source of inspiration for him. The first part of this book was still seen as "an excellent introduction" to the caste issue (1969: vii).

One must question, however, how Dumont harmonized Bouglé's conceptions with one of the initial concerns of *Homo Hierarchicus*, namely the need to examine "preconceived ideas". In fact, the thesis of the *Essays* was an illustration of self-reference, asserted by means of systematic inversions: "progress" in Europe *versus* Indian "backwardness" and "immobility"; intrinsic "solidarity" *versus* "lack of integration"; "political unity" *versus* "dispersion"; "liberty" *versus* "subjugation"; "secularism" *versus* "religion hypnosis" – and, of course, "egalitarianism" *versus* "hierarchy".

Dumont did not discuss these perspectives. As a matter of fact, his own conception of Indian society is itself "the reverse image of the West" (Toffin 1999: 9). He postulated the opposition between two social types: one, corresponding to the Western model, favours egalitarianism and individualism; the other, related to traditional societies, acknowledges hierarchy and the subordination of elements to the whole as supreme values. This was taken for granted: "As opposed to modern society, traditional societies (…) *know nothing* of equality and liberty as values, (…) *know nothing*, in short, of the individual" (1980: 8, italics added).

At first glance, the author admitted, this opposition might seem radical: "Is there not as much distance between, say, French and German modern ideologies as between Indian and Chinese traditional ideologies?" (1977 b: 8). Deep ideological differences between India and China could not be ignored; nevertheless, the author insisted, they were both holistic, although in different ways. By thus overlooking their disparities, Dumont wanted to focus on what he conceived as a main sociological difference, summarized as follows: "Chinese, Japanese, and Indian ideologies are holistic while our is individualistic" (*ibid.*: 9). In other words, from "our" point of view the former appeared uniform: "compared to us, they are similar" (*comparées à nous elles sont semblables*). Such uniformity stems from an ideological assumption, a pre-conceived similitude which is supposed to set *us* apart. A nuance should therefore be introduced into the discussion of "our preconceived ideas". The formula "we always start from ourselves" must be completed. "Our reality" is not only an inevitable *starting point* but also the means by which "our" *point of arrival* will be shaped.

Here, as in Bouglé's *Essays*, the main reference, the very basis of comparison, is Western egalitarianism – an illusory singularity rooted in ideological premises. In this regard, André Béteille observed,

> *[t]he great paradox of the modern world is that everywhere men attach themselves to the principle of equality and everywhere, in their own lives as well as in the lives of others, they encounter the presence of inequality. The more strongly they attach themselves to the principle or the ideology of equality the more oppressive the reality becomes"* (1977: 1).

***

To declare himself faithful to Risley's ideas on caste hierarchy, Bouglé adopted an unscientific attitude not acknowledged by Dumont, who saw in his own work the culmination of an academic tradition exemplarily represented by the *Essays*. As we read in *Homo Hierarchicus*,

> *To fix our ideas we must have an initial definition. Let us take Bouglé's and say that the caste system divides the whole society into a large number of hereditary groups, distinguished from one another and connected together by three characteristics:-* separation *in matters of marriage and contact, whether direct or indirect (food);* division *of labour (...); and finally* hierarchy, *which ranks the groups as relatively superior or inferior to one another* (1980: 21).

It turns out, however, that the so-called "integral definition" of the *Essays* was not adopted without profound changes being introduced. The listing of the terms "separation", "division of labour" and "hierarchy" is a preliminary re-ordering of Bouglé's three principles ("repulsion", "hierarchy", "hereditary specialization"). "Repulsion" was replaced with "separation". But Dumont's "separation" and Bouglé's "repulsion" are not equivalent.

"Separation" referred to "matters of marriage and contact", while "repulsion" concerned avoidance coloured by intense negative emotions: indifference, contempt, disgust, jealousy and hostility – states of mind encouraging isolation, withdrawal into oneself. Bouglé's "repulsion" was a problem in itself because it not only implied the implausible idea of a society based on hatred and antagonism; it also appeared to be in conflict with the two other principles, "hierarchy" and "hereditary specialization".

The exacerbated spirit of exclusivism generated by "repulsion" was supposed to stimulate feelings of selfishness justifying, among members of a caste, demands for a privileged place "in the social hierarchy". Bouglé himself observed that the intensity of feelings keeping castes separated made it difficult "to discern the outlines of (…) hierarchy" (1971: 87). If each group asserted its irreducible specificity, how could a common perspective be conceived? "How can one establish the respective places of such heterogeneous elements on one scale of respect"? (*ibid.*). The author was unable to solve the problem.

Similar difficulties arose with regard to "hereditary specialization". Professional specialization generally implies collaboration. But not in India: here, collaboration was rebuffed by "repulsion". The notion of hereditary "professional specialization" – as understood by Bouglé in the context of Indian civilization – was inseparable from that of repulsion. It implied the limitations imposed by family, caste and religion. Professional learning remained confined to the family sphere, the son perpetuating the functions of the father. And "if the custom has continued in India longer than elsewhere, it is because India has grafted a religious obligation on to a material necessity" (*ibid.*: 163). Speaking of hereditary specialization amounted to evoking a world within which individuals, families and castes remained stubbornly isolated. We have seen (Chapter 7) that, according to Bouglé, the professional specialization of Hindus bore little resemblance to the Western division of labour. The latter was dominated by a spirit of collaboration which was not supposed to exist in the former. It is clear that by referring to a "division of labour", Dumont had distanced himself from Bouglé on an essential point.

A new reformulation of Bouglé's "integral definition" was taken up later in *Homo Hierarchicus*. Castes were again declared distinct *and* connected – distinct *but* connected. However, new shades of meaning were noticeable. Consider the following passage:

> *According to [Bouglé], the caste system is composed of hereditary groups (...) which are both distinguished from one another and connected together in three ways:*
>
> *1) by gradation of status or hierarchy;*
>
> *2) by detailed rules aimed at ensuring their separation;*
>
> *3) by* division of labour and the interdependence which results from it (1980: 43, italics added).

This time, "hierarchy" was presented as the first element of the series. The last place was now assigned to the "division of labour and the interdependence which results from it". It is no longer necessary to emphasize that the idea of *interdependence* was alien to the argument of the *Essays*. The opposite had been stated. Mutual indifference, the "instinctive" mutual disdain due to which collaboration proved impossible in India, had been underlined instead (Bouglé 1971: 169).

Before the publication of *Homo Hierarchicus*, Dumont had already mentioned *interdependence* as a decisive aspect of the Indian system: "In India, the separation and hierarchy of castes only make sense because everyone knows, without needing to say it, that the society is based on the *interdependence* of castes" (1975 [1964]: 17-8, our translation). Claiming in *Homo*

Hierarchicus that *interdependence* arose from the notion of division of labour, Dumont showed that he had read the *Essays* in terms which *were not* those of their author.

Bouglé's "integral definition" of the caste system had been radically recreated: "separation" had replaced "repulsion"; and "hereditary specialization", transmuted into a perfect replica of the Western division of labour, was dominated by relations of *interdependence*. Distinction *and* connection were seen by Dumont as simultaneously at work in the caste system. Bouglé had stated nothing of the sort.

***

The idea of "repulsion" was partially recovered at the end of *Homo Hierarchicus*; again, this was done in a way that was entirely foreign to the spirit of the *Essays*. The supposed "strong tendency" of a caste to split and give rise to new groups was addressed by Dumont in a section of Chapter 9: "Bouglé postulated a reciprocal 'repulsion' whereby groups would be separated from each other like particles charged with electricity of the same sign, and would probably explain their fissiparity in this way" (*ibid.* 197). Bouglé's metaphor of the elder-pith ball was *unrelated to the question of caste fissiparity*. It was nothing but a new trope on *permanent incommunicability* – the only suitable perspective in the light of the reiterated conceptions of the *Essays*. Unexpectedly assuming that the image of particles with identical electrical charges would fit *exceptional disruptive* situations, Dumont conferred to the concept of "repulsion" a sociological plausibility it did not possess. Emptying it of its original meaning or, at least, limiting its scope (as in the passage just considered), he adopted a cautious attitude. It was only to the extent that Dumont discarded – fully or partially – the notion of "repulsion" that he could credit Bouglé with the idea that castes were "distinguished from one another *and* connected together" (1980: 21, italics added).

II

Dumont asserted at the beginning of *Homo Hierarchicus* that the "true" hierarchy is not fully recognized by modern man. He did not fail to refer to "our" current vision of hierarchy to better show that it does not conform to the reality of castes:

> *Starting from our current view of hierarchy we tend at first to picture the caste system (...) as a linear order going from the highest to the lowest, a transitive non-cyclic order: each caste is lower than those which precede it and higher than those which follow it and they are all comprised between two extreme points* (ibid.: 39).

This was an unsatisfactory perspective, as Srinivas himself had stressed: "in the middle region in particular it is often difficult to rank one of two given castes absolutely in relation to the other" (*ibid.*.).

In contradiction with modern thinking, therefore, linearity had to be banned from hierarchy. It was necessary to return to the original meaning of the notion, calling attention to "the *principles* whereby the castes are ranked in a more or less exact order". Beneath the surface, "a system of oppositions, a structure" could be found (*ibid.*).

At that point, Dumont introduced a reflection on "structure", placing the opposition between the traditional and the modern at the centre of the discussion: unlike modern societies, traditional ones favour the whole, whose elements are apprehended "as the product of (a) network of relations". He recalled the lesson of phonology – a phoneme is nothing but "the other of others" – and stressed that the *interdependence* of the elements had to be given priority (*ibid.*: 40). Also in this regard, a pioneering role was ascribed to Bouglé. But which particular aspect of his work did Dumont refer to? Was it the one he had submitted to his own reinterpretation? Or was it, on the contrary, the one postulating the radical disjunction implied in the concept of "repulsion"? Dumont was not sure. In one passage, he alluded to Bouglé as someone ahead of his time, an author who "had started from the system instead of the element" (*ibid.*: 35). In another, he placed him among the writers who had a tendency to "emphasize separation". Bouglé, he then wrote, had "assumed a 'repulsion' which automatically kept the castes apart from one another. All said and done, even where the intention was to treat caste as part of a whole, the tendency to treat each caste as a small self-sufficient society was not completely overcome" (*ibid.*: 30).

In fact, the term "system" was unsuitable for characterizing the reality described by Bouglé: the spirit of caste was "designed to atomize the societies into which it penetrates; it divides them (…) into a multitude of opposed fragments; it brings each of their elementary groups face to face, separated by a mutual repulsion" (Bouglé 1971: 9). One does not see how a structural perspective could apprehend a reality presented as definitively divided – so deeply divided that no relationship whatsoever was conceivable between its parts. To separate, to distinguish, to cut ties – Dumont insisted – was the propensity of the modern turn of mind, rendering the caste system incomprehensible to Westerners: "As soon as we hear of human groups which separate themselves, distinguish themselves, isolate themselves fiercely from one another, we believe we know what we have to deal with. (…) Well, nothing is more false" (Dumont 1980: 40-1).

Bouglé – an avant-garde author in Dumont's opinion – had thought differently. But let us look at what he actually wrote:

> *When we say that the spirit of caste reigns in a society, we mean that the different groups of which that society is composed, repel each other rather than attract, that each retires within itself, isolates itself, makes every effort to prevent its members from*

> *contracting alliances or even from entering into relations with neighbouring groups* (1971: 9).

The "innovative" point of view that Dumont attributed to Bouglé exactly reproduced the arguments he had criticized.

III

Like Srinivas, Dumont deemed it necessary to order the wide range of criteria used by castes to differentiate themselves from each other. Once again, he only had to adopt a practice attributed to Bouglé: "to reduce things to their principles while omitting nothing essential" (1980: 43). Having first associated each of the principles of his "integral definition" with a different cause, Bouglé had ended up basing them all together on "the opposition between the pure and the impure". This was the view adopted in *Homo Hierarchicus*: the relation between pure and impure was the *fundamental opposition* of the caste system (*ibid.*: 30).

The Brahmin personified the ideal of purity; and since pure / impure commonly characterizes the opposition Brahmins / Untouchables, Dumont assumed it was tacitly applied to any other relationship: "it is by implicit reference to this opposition that the society of castes appears consistent and rational to those who live in it" (*ibid.*: 44).

In order to illustrate the spirit of the method to be followed, he began by evoking – quite significantly! – criteria of distinction that highlighted the Brahmins' ideal of purity: (1) the vegetarian diet, often adopted by Brahmins, is commonly considered a sign of purity; (2) the prohibition of divorce and the remarriage of widows are characteristic of Brahminic behaviour and therefore marks of purity. He then supposed the members of a caste, declaring: "We are vegetarians, which places us above X, Y, Z, who eat meat; but we allow the remarriage of widows, which places us below A, B, C, who forbid it" (*ibid.*: 56-7). Two sets of imaginary groups of unequal status (A, B, C / X, Y, Z, superior and inferior respectively) were thus formed: "to say 'we are vegetarians' is to unite oneself with all vegetarian castes and oppose oneself to all the others" (*ibid.*: 57). Through this process, the members of the caste in question would distinguish themselves from those considered higher and from those considered lower. A series of similar dichotomies would allow a caste to be ranked: "It can well be imagined", Dumont went on to say, "that it is difficult to grade all the castes of a given area in a fixed hierarchical order *even though the fundamental principle is beyond question and universal in its operation*" (*ibid.*, italics added). Hindrances would be removed if the different criteria were reduced to the message they were all supposed to convey: the pure / impure opposition; the superiority of the pure over the impure.

This is questionable. The admission of impurity by one caste vis-à-vis another is far from obvious. As often observed, even a low caste "may deny that it displays low caste characteristics or that the characteristics it displays are indicative of low rank" (Berreman 1965: 121). Noting the "complication" which results from the wide range of criteria "and from the necessity of evaluating them in relation to each other", Dumont acknowledged that each caste "manipulate(s) this situation to its advantage" (1980: 57). The claim of particular criteria regarding distinction is a major instrument for the definition of a group's identity. But the sociological relevance of this process is devalued by the assertion that "in people's consciousness *all* the criteria of distinction appear as so many different forms of the same principle" (*ibid.*: 57, italics added) – that is, the opposition between the pure and the impure.

***

Many ethnographic examples show that the nature of social relations is not only masked but distorted by the postulate of the superiority of the pure over the impure. The facts collected and examined by Gloria Raheja are expressive in this regard.

In Pahansu, a village in Uttar Pradesh, the Gujars are the "dominant" landholding *jati*. The services provided to them throughout the year by different castes are paid in kind, according to the traditional *jajmani* system. These payments differ clearly from small donations (*dan*) that Brahmins and others castes *have to accept* at specific times and under certain circumstances. A donor transfers in this way to a recipient some kind of individual or collective inauspiciousness, manifested in different forms: illness, madness, infertility… The Gujars never accept such donations but constantly take the initiative to free themselves of their own inauspiciousness through "poisoned gifts" which they offer to Brahmins, Barbers and Untouchables in particular. Although these people are privileged recipients of donations from the Gujars, they are in no way distinguished by the latter according to social status. One can thus understand Raheja's allusion to the "contextual equivalence" of the members of these castes" (1988: 35) and, of course, her scepticism towards Dumont's conceptions:

> *In giving priority to the ideology of hierarchy, particularly to the opposition of the pure and the impure, it is of course impossible for Dumont (...) to acknowledge that the ritual services performed by the "pure" Brahman and the "impure" Washermen and Barbers could in any way be religiously equivalent* (ibid.: 26).

Raheja sometimes felt that, in this context, the world of caste hierarchy "had been turned topsy-turvy" (*ibid.*: 32). This certainly means that she did not intend to question the generally accepted views: a hierarchy turned upside-down is still a hierarchy, after all… But her reflections allowed new questions to be asked. If the hierarchical presupposition underpinned Raheja's field research, the answers she obtained did not fail to surprise. When asked about "the hierarchical considerations involved in giving and receiving", the Gujars approached the matter in conjectural terms which did not really arouse their interest (*ibid.*: 242). In Pahansu, she writes, the social relationships "may be ordered in terms other than rank and the opposition of purity and impurity". She admits that two orders of social relations – and two orders of criteria – coexist side by side: "The order of castes grounded in rank or hierarchy and that grounded in what I have termed the centrality of the dominant caste of *jajmāns* (…) are acted upon in distinct contexts of village social life" (*ibid.*: 29). But should one postulate unrelated levels of reality? Is it conceivable that Brahmins and Untouchables, symbolically associated as recipients of the inauspicious gifts of the dominant caste, would not be led to question the very nature of their relationship?

IV

It was in the third Chapter of *Homo Hierarchicus* that a definition of "true" hierarchy was presented. Some of its aspects had already been discussed. Dumont established, on the one hand, that linearity should not be presumed; and, on the other, that the opposition between the pure and the impure was the cornerstone of the pre-modern concept. These arguments should have supported his redefinition of hierarchy.

The opposition between the pure and the impure was declared to be religious in nature and this was also insistently emphasized. Hierarchy, Dumont wrote, is "the *principle by which the elements of a whole are ranked in relation to the whole*, it being understood that in the majority of societies it is religion which provides the view of the whole" (*ibid.*: 66). This idea was foreign to modern man.

But the religious perspective requires, in the author's conception, a classification of beings "according to their degree of dignity" (*ibid.*: 65); it implies, in other words, the linear arrangement Dumont wanted to eliminate. It was, therefore, necessary to look in a different direction. This time, Dumont adopted the point of view of Georges Dumézil who had noted in 1948 that the traditional hierarchy of the four *varnas* was "linear in appearance only". The Brahmins, although opposed to the Kshatriyas, made up with them the "two forces" (*ubhe virye*) and were clearly distinguished from the Vaishyas. Taken, in turn, as a cohesive set, the *dvija*, or "twice-born" – Brahmins, Kshatriyas and Vaishyas – were opposed to Shudras.

The theory of the *varnas* would account for the non-linearity of caste society. But to achieve this result, the author was forced to ignore the opposition between the pure and the impure which he had considered essential. As he could not fail to emphasize, the organization of the *varnas* "is a hierarchy other than that of the pure and the impure" (*ibid.*: 66). This is not the most important aspect to consider. As a matter of fact, *nothing typically pre-modern* characterized the perspective adopted by Dumézil, for whom the *varnas* form a sequence "rather Hegelian in character, in which a thesis summons an antithesis then combines with it in synthesis that becomes in turn a further thesis" (1988 [1948]: 65). Briefly, in his quest for a non-linear hierarchy, Dumont had taken a puzzling detour, emphasizing *an unequivocally modern configuration*.

V

The succession of Dumézil's nested dichotomies corresponds, in Dumont's terminology, to the "encompassment of the contrary" (1980: 76): castes were said to form "hierarchical oppositions" – relationships where the "higher" term not only *encompassed* a "lower" one (or lower ones) but was also supposed to represent the set of the groups involved.

Unexpectedly, once again, Dumont admitted that this conception could already be found in *modern* Western thought. Reviewing the way hierarchy had been addressed from the beginning of the 20th century, he first alluded to the work of Risley as Census Commissioner. Risley had intended to arrive at a "classification of castes" – "a laudable undertaking" in spite of "its drawbacks and limitations" (*ibid.*: 79). We already know that Risley's effort did not result in a "classification of *castes*"; what he proposed was an inconsistent hierarchy of large groups into which castes were introduced. But Dumont credited him with having adopted what he considered to be the golden rule for analysing and bringing order to a multifaceted reality: he had the "merit of throwing into relief the markedly different ways in which a universal principle was applied in different Provinces" (*ibid.*). This emerged from the lists of social precedence drawn up throughout the census operations. Setting side by side the lists concerning Bengal and Madras, one could conclude that, despite differences between the north and the south, the categories into which castes had been divided were based "on a series of hierarchical oppositions" (*ibid.*: 80) – similar sequences that obeyed the same principle, defined from the point of view of the Brahmins, the reference group (*ibid.*: 81).

What exactly were the *hierarchical oppositions* just referred to? To answer this question, we need to see how Dumont referred to the caste groups of Bengal Proper, presented by Risley in the general report of 1903. A short preliminary note is necessary here. A first list had been drawn up by Risley himself and entrusted to Gait. It was just a draft and Gait submitted it to "committees of Native gentlemen appointed for the purpose" (Gait 1902: 368) Their criticisms were taken into account but the final "precedence table" still raised numerous problems. Gait did not try to hide the insurmountable differences of opinion that remained among the members of the committees. The difficulty of the task accounted for the poverty of the outcome, as acknowledged in his report on *The Lower Provinces of Bengal and their Feudatories* (1902). Extensively (but not always fully) reproducing Gait's classification, Risley minimized the obstacles inherent in the process, simply stating that the data compiled by him had been adopted "after careful examination by local committees of native gentlemen".

If it is true that Risley simplified and reconfigured Gait's text, it is no less clear that Dumont simplified and reconfigured Risley's. For Dumont did not limit himself to reproducing the data published by Risley; he reorganized them in the spirit of his own conceptions.

The first of the seven classes of Bengal Proper – labelled "Bráhmans" by Gait (see Chapter 6, Table 14) – included a heterogeneous series of castes, some with a very low status: "As everyone knows, there are Bráhmans and Bráhmans", Risley wrote. It would be pointless to specify, for instance, the exact social position of the Vysokta Brahmins, because they ranked "so low that even their own clients will not touch food in their houses" (Risley in Risley and Gait 1903: 540). Dumont did not find it necessary to mention their existence. He limited himself to noting that, in Bengal, Brahmins come first (1980: 80). Being in his opinion the epitome of purity, the Brahmins in general were the main encompassing group, representatives of the whole of Hindu society. For him, the first "hierarchical opposition" was the relationship Brahmins / non Brahmins, the first level of a taxonomic tree with no correspondence in Risley's text:

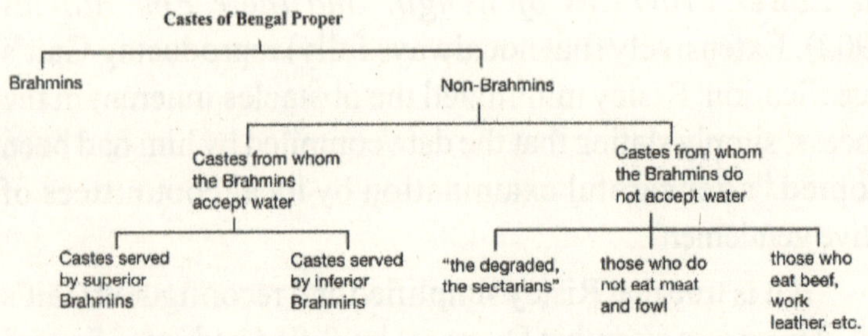

Table 21 : *Schematic representation of the castes of Bengal Proper as reorganized by Dumont, 1980: 79*

According to Dumont, non-Brahmins were in turn divided into two groups: those from whom the Brahmins "accept water, and those from whom they do not" (Dumont 1980: 79). This synthesized the current idea of Brahmins' supremacy. For wherever Gait and Risley had spoken of groups whose water was accepted or refused by *higher castes*, Dumont always spoke of groups whose water was accepted or refused by *Brahmins*.

Dumont's group made up of those from whom the Brahmins accept water was subdivided into:

(a) castes served by superior Brahmins; and

(b) castes served by inferior Brahmins.

Castes served by superior Brahmins included Risley's second and third classes – respectively referred to by Gait as "Other castes ranking above clean Sudras"; and "Clean Sudras". None of them was arranged in an indisputable order. "Other castes ranking above clean Sudras" were formed by Rajputs – not indigenous to Bengal – followed by Vaidyas (physicians) and Kayasths (writers). Gait had observed that no disputes on "caste precedence were so violent or so acrimonious as those regarding the conflicting claims of each of these two castes to rank above the other" (1902: 370). The relative positions of "Clean Sudras" were not any clearer: some observers considered that one of them could just as well have been placed at the bottom of the second Class (*ibid.*).

Risley's fourth class ("Clean Castes with degraded Bráhmans" in Gait's terminology) was composed of only two groups. Their water was accepted by "high castes" but the condition of their Brahmins was degraded (Risley in Risley and Gait 1903: 541). This was a misleading description, as we have seen (Chapter 6): according to Gait himself, not all high castes accepted water from certain members of this class; and not all members of this class were served by degraded priests (1902: 371). Risley did not mention such "exceptions"; Gait's text, if taken into account, would have made Dumont's taxonomic tree problematic (not no say ineffectual).

The fifth class – "Castes lower than the above whose water is not usually taken" (Gait) – involved the same fallacy, shown this time by Risley himself. It included Baishtam (aggregating members of different castes converted to Vaishnavism), Sunari and Subarnabanik. This last caste deserves particular attention. Although despised by clean Shudras, they declared themselves to be descendants of the ancient Vaishyas, and Vaidik Brahmins accepted their water (Rislcy in Risley and Gait 1903: 542). In Dumont's laconic words, they were designated as "the degraded, the sectarians", a sub-division of "[those] from whom the Brahmans do not accept water" (1980: 80). The ill-defined character of a class composed of those from whom, in Risley's words, "the higher castes do not *usually* take water" (Risley in Risley and Gait 1903: 541, italics added) was thus considered irrelevant.

Class six – "Low castes who abstain from beef, pork, and fowls" (Gait) – encompasses a long list of units which, "in the original draft, were distributed over four separate groups" (Gait

1902: 372). Their heterogeneous character led again to contradictions: the Rájabansi of North Bengal comprised distinct classes, "the better of which (…) are served by Bráhmans who are not degraded". According to some observers, they should be placed somewhere … between classes three and four. This was not an isolated case: "There is a sub-caste of Sukli in Midnapore (…) which is served by good Utkal Bráhmans" and should be ranked in class four (1902: 373) – where, in disarray, castes whose water was accepted by certain "high castes" but refused by others were placed, as well as castes served sometimes by good Brahmins, sometimes by degraded ones.

Finally, class seven, "the lowest grade of the Bengal system", comprised those "who eat all manner of unclean food" (Risley in Risley and Gait 1903: 543).

***

The beautiful regularity that emerges from Table 21 was obtained at the cost of unacceptable distortions. The numerous difficulties reported by Gait were deliberately concealed or minimized by Risley, who intended to preserve the credibility of his thesis on social precedence. Dumont did nothing different. Transforming Risley's text or omitting some of its information, he tried to safeguard by similar means the coherence of his own perspectives on *hierarchical oppositions*. Only wrong inferences made it possible to transform Risley's classification into a taxonomic tree.

In 1979, in his "Postface" to the "Tel" edition of *Homo Hierarchicus*, Dumont made it clear that the caste hierarchy should not be formalized as a taxonomic tree: "I believe that hierarchy is not, essentially, a chain of superimposed commands, nor even a chain of beings of decreasing dignity, nor yet a taxonomic tree, but a relation that can succinctly be called 'the encompassing of the contrary'" (1980: 239). The hierarchical opposition, the relation between encompassing and encompassed, was considered "just as indispensable to structural thought as the distinctive opposition or relation of complementariness of older standing" (*ibid.*: 243). But he stressed the resistance to which it had been subjected: "it is surprising that so little note has hitherto been taken of it" (*ibid.*).

In relation to Risley's work, the notion of hierarchical opposition appears, however, on two occasions. We know the first one. Risley was *applauded* for having recognized the "universal principle" behind different hierarchical contexts, each of them conceived as a series of "hierarchical oppositions" (*ibid.*: 80). In the second case, Risley was *blamed*. This time, he had supposed that "hierarchy consisted in a linear order", not seeing that "this order was only the consequence (...) of a hierarchical opposition: a single opposition so far as its principle is concerned, but indefinitely diversified and segmented according to circumstance, region, etc." (*ibid.*: 81-2).

Both praise and blame are unjustified. In order to assert that the caste groups had been accurately "based on (...) hierarchical oppositions", Dumont arbitrarily rearranged Risley's data. Even more unexpected, though, is the nature of his criticism. How could Risley have apprehended hierarchy as a non-linear order? His perspective had even been reinforced and "legitimized" by the racial theory, towards which Dumont had shown himself to be quite complacent: "on the extent that each caste constitutes more or less perfectly a demographically isolated unit, it is natural that the average physical characteristics of its members should differ from those of another caste" (*ibid.*: 28).

The retrospective use of the concept of hierarchical opposition could only prove inadequate. From a certain point of view, Dumont's attitude towards Risley evokes his rereading of Bouglé's *Essays*. In both cases, an ancestor was revisited and his thoughts were recreated. Dumont reshaped somehow the tradition of which he claimed to be the heir.

CHAPTER-10

AGAINST EVIDENCE FINAL THOUGHTS

I

The idea of caste hierarchy, accepted with greater or lesser conviction, has a recent history. Until the end of the 19th century, Hindu society was perceived as a chaotic reality by most Europeans, including those who lived in India for long periods of time.

Bernard Cohn had a different perspective: "The earliest direct observers of the Indian caste system in modern times were Portuguese adventurers, administrators, merchants and priests", some of whom "naively but accurately reported major cultural features of the caste system which continue to be recognized as central today" (1990 [1968]: 139). Duarte Barbosa (1480-1521) was one of them. Shortly before his death, he had written a long account of his experience of India over the course of two decades. A first English translation of this text, undertaken from a Spanish version by Henry Stanley, appeared in 1866. The second one, authored by Mansel Longworth Dames, was published in two volumes (1918 and 1921). Cohn was acquainted with both. He generally followed Stanley's translation (sometimes considered more suitable) but was indebted to Dames' extensive notes.

"Striking in Barbosa's description", Cohn stressed, "is his matter-of-fact and objective approach". Believing that his account only expressed "what he saw and what he was told", Cohn thought he could trust the author's depiction of the caste system – "organized as a hierarchy with Brahmans on top and Untouchables at the bottom" (1990: 140). Was this really the traveller's point of view? Here is his first allusion to Hindu society:

> *[B]efore this kingdom of Guzerate fell into the hands of the Moors, a certain race of Heathen whom the Moors call* Resbutos *dwelt therein, who in those days were the knights and wardens of the land and made war wheresoever it was needful* (Barbosa [Dames] 1918: 109-110).

"Resbutos", a corruption of Rājpūts (King's sons), was the term designating the representatives of the military class. They were followed by the "Baneanes" [Baniya], "merchants and traders" (*ibid.*: 110-111) who "[eat] neither flesh nor fish, nor anything subject to death; they slay nothing, nor are they willing even to see the slaughter of any animal" (*ibid.*: 111); "in their houses they sup by daylight, for neither by night nor by day will they light a lamp, by reason of certain little flies which perish in the flame thereof" (*ibid.*: 112). Such features were suited to the Jain, to whom the Baniya were sometimes assimilated.

Only then were the Brahmins referred to: "[T]here is here another class of Heathen whom they call *Bramenes*, who are priests among them and persons who manage and rule their houses of prayer and idol-worship" (*ibid.*: 114-115). Barbosa noted that

> *[they] have in their creed many resemblances to the Holy Trinity, and hold in great honour the relation of the Triune Three, and always make their prayers to God, whom they (...) adore as the true God, Creator*

and maker of all things, who is three persons and one God (ibid.: 115).

1. "Resbutos" (*Rajputs*);
2. "Baneanes" (*Baniyas*: merchants and traders);
3. "Bramenes" (*Brahmins*).

Table 22: *Barbosa's "three divisions" of Hindu society (Gujarat).*

Dames admitted he was in the presence of a faithful description here: the traveller had divided "the Hindus into three main sections, Resbutos, Baneanes and Bramanes, that is Rājputs, Banyāns and Brāhmans, a very accurate statement of the broader features of their organization" (*ibid.*: 110, note 1).

This is an unexpected comment, for Barbosa had shown that he was aware of the complexity of the Hindu social system: in Gujarat "are woven white cotton fabrics both fine and coarse, and other printed in patterns; also much silk cloth and coloured velvets of poor quality, velvety satins and taffeties, also thick carpets" (*ibid.*: 141); "many craftsmen of mechanic trades in cunning work of many kinds" could likewise be found (*ibid.*) – "workers in stones, and makers of false stones and pearls of divers sorts which appear to be real; also very good goldsmiths who do very fine work" (*ibid.*: 142).

***

The Book of Duarte Barbosa provides abundant examples of the tendency to "translate" the Indian reality into European terms: "In the great and fair city called Cambaya (...) [there are] many fair houses, very lofty, with windows and roofed with tiles in our manner" (*ibid.:* 140) – "covered with roofs in the Spanish fashion" (Barbosa [Stanley] 1866: 64); Indian craftsmen make works of many sorts "as in Flanders" (Barbosa [Dames] 1918: 141). The Brahmins offered, of course, the most obvious pretext for comparison: "Wheresoever they find our churches enter them and make prayers and adorations to our Images, always asking for Santa Maria, like men who have some knowledge and understanding of these matters" (*ibid.*: 116). Remarks of this kind abound in the text. Should we not presume that the traveller had also unconsciously "described" Gujarat society according to a model inspired by the West?

Let us now turn to Vijayanagar (Narsinga), the Empire that, at the time, occupied almost entirely the southern part of the subcontinent. Here too, a set of three social classes was mentioned (*ibid.*: 212). "The principal of these is that of the King, the great Lords, the knights and fighting men" (*ibid.*: 213). The second was represented by Brahmins, "who are priests and rulers of their houses of worship" (*ibid.*: 217). The last was a "class of folk very like unto the Bramenes, who wear round their necks certain cords of twisted silk, from which hangs a cloth bag containing a stone the size of an egg, which they say is their god" (*ibid.*: 217-18). Dames recognized in them the Lingayats. They were merchants and traders, going "everywhere in safety taking goods from one kingdom to another…" (*ibid.*: 218):

1. King, great lords and fighting men;
2. Brahmins;
3. Merchants and traders.

Table 23: *The "three classes of Heathen"* (Vijayanagar).

In spite of the similarities observed (Tables 22 and 23), the author no longer considered that the series of Vijayanagar corresponded to "actual caste divisions": it was "such as would be likely to strike an observer from Europe" – (1) the King and nobility; (2) priests; and (3) an important class of merchants and traders (Barbosa [Dames] 1918: 212, note 3).

As before, representatives of political power occupy the highest rank. One cannot fail to see that this is reminiscent of the Indo-European trifunctional ideology studied by Georges Dumézil. It supposed that there was collaboration between representatives of three "functions": (1) sovereignty (in terms of both its magical and its juridical aspects); (2) warfare, protection of people and territory; and (3) economy in the broad sense of the term (agriculture, pastoralism and so on). The reappearance of such conceptions in the European traditions of the Middle Ages was carefully analised by Georges Duby.

II

The oldest examples of social tripartition in the medieval West date back to the second half of the 9th century. The formula *sacerdotes, milites, agricolae*, credited to the Benedictine monk Haymo of Auxerre corresponds to that attributed to Alfred the Great, King of Wessex – *gebedmen, fyrdmen, weorcmen* ("men of prayer", "men of war", "men of labour").

The tenacity of this structure is notorious even though the relative position of the three classes did not remain constant. The canonical formula granted the highest ranking to priesthood, but by the end of the 12th century, a change had occurred. In the *Estoire des ducs de Normadie*, written around 1180 by Benedict of Sainte-Maure, *the nobility preceded the clergy*: knights, clerics and villains. From then on, the two formulas coexisted, although the nobility gradually tended to occupy the highest rank.

In one way or another, the medieval European theory of the "three orders" remained as *an ideal of stability*, a commonplace sometimes considered suitable even in partial descriptions of non-European societies. Suffice it to recall the synthetic account of the Persian society by Jean-Baptiste Tavernier:

> *The State of* Persia *is distinguish'd like most of the* European *States, into three Bodies. The first is that of the Sword, which answers to the Nobility, and comprehends the Kings houshold, the* Kans, *and all the Souldiery. The second is that of the Quill, comprehending all those that belong to the Law and the Courts of Justice. The third is compos'd of Merchants, Handicraftsmen and Labourers* (1678, V, IX).

Like this excerpt from Tavernier's work, Barbosa's passages on Gujarat and Vijayanagar testify to the symbolic power of the medieval tradition. We can only emphasize once again the unfounded nature of Cohn's considerations of Barbosa's "matter-of-fact and objective approach".

The influence of the medieval conceptions concerning the "three orders" or "three estates" led to significant aspects of Indian reality being disregarded. It is remarkable that Barbosa ignored the importance of agriculture in the subcontinent's economy. But, by including merchants in the tripartite schemes and excluding peasants therefrom, he again complied with European premises: the gradual rise of merchants in late medieval society had made the peasant – the *villain* – a despicable figure.

Relating this time the "main" classes of Hindu society to the "three orders" of the medieval European tradition, Dames seemed to believe that the traveller had implicitly postulated that there was a homology between hierarchical social structures. But no hint of a *concrete social organization* can be abstracted from the old tripartite ideology. As clarified by Dumézil and emphasized by Duby, this tripartition is indeed an abstract, speculative classification with no direct correspondence with the "real" society: when someone had "to be celebrated in panegyric" it was common to resort to this stereotype, echoes of which "abound in countless biographies, both real and fictitious" (Duby 1980: 6). However, Duby added,

> *this model [was] rarely applied in an explicit way to the body social. The 'tripartite ideology' (...) is the backbone of a value system; overt use is made of it in myth, epic, and flattery; but ordinarily it remains latent, unformulated; only rarely is it brought into the open in the shape of imperious statements as to the proper ideal of society, order, i.e., power* (ibid.).

It is as the evocation of a purely *ideal* classification that Barbosa's examples must be understood. Let us now return to the tripartite structure of Gujarat.

Barbosa began by going back to the time of the Muslim conquest: "In ancient days this kingdom pertained to the Heathen, and the Moors took it from them in war, so that the King thereof is at this present time a Moor" (Barbosa [Dames]: 108-09). He did not deal with the fact that the Ruler of Gujarat was now "a Moor". Apparently, he just intended to recall the coherence of an ideal model which had been destroyed. Political authority, the keystone of the tripartite structure as seen by him, could in no way be assigned to a Muslim. Instead, the heirs of the comrades in arms of the dethroned King were placed at the first level of the triad. The ancient Rajputs had sought refuge in the mountains, where their descendants still kept large villages under their control: they were "very fine horsemen, and good archers", always at war against the Muslim rulers, because they had "no king or lord over them" (*ibid.*: 110).

It is clear that the tripartite structure of Gujarat says nothing about Hindu society. It merely built a bridge between a blurred past and the traveller's present – it was a *timeless ideal order*, represented in purely European terms. The model that Cohn thought he had seen in Barbosa's text – a caste system with Brahmins at the top and Untouchables at the base – was obviously not confirmed by any of the previous examples.

III

Consider now the part of the account that relates to Malabar. In Dames' words, "of all the countries dealt with by Barbosa, Malabar exceeds the rest in interest, as it was here that, owing to his long residence and his acquaintance with the language of the people, he was able to give a really full and accurate description of their inhabitants, their customs and their elaborate caste-system" (in Barbosa 1921: xxiv). The traveller's testimony would be of inestimable value: "The structure of society in this corner of India continues almost unaltered at the present day, and it is possible therefore to test the accuracy of his observations on the caste system by comparison with that still existing" (*ibid.*).

But let us refer directly to Barbosa's text: "You must know that in all Malabar there are eighteen castes of Native Heathen" (*ibid.*: 7). They were successively described, starting with a long reference to the Sovereigns of the country, the unambiguous focus of the author's scrutiny. Everything about them seemed important, mainly of course the rules regarding matrilineal descent.

The King of Calicut deserved special attention. Endowed with incomparable prestige, he was given the title Zamorin, a particular distinction. The passages about him are among the most detailed in the text. But it is clear that Barbosa was interested in every aspect of life at court and the mechanisms of kingship. A vivid description was given of the period between the death of a Zamorin and the enthronement of his successor, a time of apparent lethargy whose symbolic importance was appropriately underlined.

After the cremation of a King, a period of thirteen days of grief began. The kingdom was ruled during this time by a nobleman of royal lineage, the heir remaining for the time being a powerless figure (*ibid.*: 12-3). This was a moment of insecurity, at the end of which social links were ritually reaffirmed. When the new King was raised to the throne, he solemnly committed to respect the old laws. "Certain counts (…) along with all the others of the royal lineage, and the grandees" swore in turn to serve him with loyalty and fidelity (Barbosa [Stanley] 1866: 08). The traveller had full perception of the relevance of such events which seemed to give the people the feeling of a return to political and social stability.

Barbosa then turned to the (Nambudiri) Brahmins. Although they were seen as enjoying "great honour among the Indians" (Barbosa [Dames] 1921: 34), the passages devoted to them were terse. It was observed that they marry only once, "in our manner". As previously noted, they "hold that there is a God in three persons". In spite of many similarities with Christianity, they had "no knowledge nor information concerning the life of our Lord Jesus Christ"; so, it seemed, "they believe and respect many truths, yet do not tell them truly". The Zamorin held them in "high esteem" and they were at his service, serving him "in every manner except in arms" (*ibid.*: 37).

The Nayars were discussed next. They had been mentioned several times in the context of their relationship to the Zamorin. But now an overview was provided: "you are to know (...) that in this land of Malabar there is [a] caste of people called Nayres, and among them are noblemen who have no other duty than to serve in war" (*ibid.*: 38). They are "very free from stain in their nobility" and punctilious with regard to contacts generating pollution (*ibid.*: 39).

The members of the Nayar military aristocracy were introduced from childhood to the demands of martial life. They lived with the King and other great Lords, and received allowances from them as soon as they became armed knights. This marked the beginning of their duties. Like the dubbing to knighthood in feudal Europe, this was a symbolic rebirth: only that ceremony made them "real" Nayars, worthy of being so named. The young men were "armed as knights by the hand of the king or lord with whom they live" (Barbosa [Stanley] 1866: 128) and, from then on, powerful "vassalage" links were established: "When these *Nayres* accept service with the King or with any other person by whom they are to be paid they bind themselves to die for him" (Barbosa [Dames] 1921: 48).

The Braberes (or Biabares)[1] were mentioned next. They "deal in goods of every kind, both in the seaports and inland, wheresoever their trade is of most profit". They are "of as pure lineage as the nairs, men and women, and they may touch one another" (Barbosa [Stanley] 1866: 134). This is the last-mentioned caste of the "honourable people" (*gentes honradas*), below which all are considered serfs of the King and other grandees (*ibid.*: 116).

The distinction between "honourable" and "low" people was frequently used and requires careful consideration. The special rights enjoyed by "honourable people" were made particularly clear in the section dealing with justice in Calicut. Except in very particular circumstances, a Nayar could not "be imprisoned or fettered for anything he may do" (Barbosa [Dames] 1921: 30). Brahmins suffered "death for no cause whatsoever, their own headman [giving] them a mild chastisement" (*ibid.*: 34). As for the privileges of the Braberes, they "are such that the King (…) cannot execute them by legal process" (*ibid.*: 56). Outlandish traders (Guzarates and Moors) benefited from the same indulgence.

---

1. A corruption of Vyāpāri, "a trading section of Nāyar" (Thurston and Rangachari 1909, Vol. VII: 412).

Carefully distinguished from the rest of the population, the castes of the so-called "honourable people" corresponded to those which made up the triads of Gujarat and Vijayanagar:

1. King and Nayars (as representatives of the military elite)
2. Brahmins
3. Traders

Table 24: *"Honourable people" of Calicut*

Barbosa noted that in Calicut the sanctions were applied "according to the qualities of the persons" (Barbosa [Stanley] 1866: 116); and that, "as there are many castes among the folk, so also do their rules vary" (Barbosa [Dames]1921: 27). Only one distinction, however, was referred to, that between "honourable people" and all the others. The former were brought together in various ways by different versions. As representatives of the military aristocracy, the Nayars usually came first but the remaining "groups were mentioned without concern for systematic ordering: "Nayares, Chatins, Guzarates, Bramanes and Brabares"; "Nayres, Chatis, Moors, Guzarates, Bramenes" (Barbosa 2000: 144). No gradation whatsoever can be inferred here.

***

As for the "low people", a preliminary observation is needed. "Low people", "low caste", and "low caste folk" are expressions commonly adopted by Dames to render the Portuguese word "*vilão*" (*villain*). Stanley usually translated it as "peasant" and, occasionally, as "low and base people".

These were general denominations for various castes as opposed to the "honourable people" – the unprotected groups whose members could be flogged in justice, tortured or even killed.

They did not form a coherent set. Potters, Washermen and Weavers stood out by virtue of their special relationships with the "honourable people", the Nayars in particular.

These special cases must be highlighted since the rules normally observed by the Nayars are very strict: "They drink no wine, they do not sleep with women of low caste (...). When they walk along a street or road they shout to the low caste folk to get out of their way" (Barbosa [Dames] 1921: 49).

However, when the Nayars go to war, "they may touch any person soever, even though they be of low caste (*vilãos*), and may eat and drink with them in their houses without bathing (as a purification)" (*ibid.*: 52).

Another exception concerned their relationships with Potters, Washermen and Weavers. We are told that the Potters (Cuiavem, Kusavan) "do not differ from the *Nayres*, yet by reason of a fault they committed, they remain separate from them" (*ibid.*: 57). The Nayars "may sleep with their women" (*ibid.*: 58).

The Washermen – who washed clothes for Kings, Brahmins and Nayars – always had with them a large quantity of cloths "as well of their own as of others"; and since "there are many *Nayres* who have no clothes of their own to wear", they "take shares with them" (*ibid.*).[2] The Washermen "do not mix with others, nor others

2. "There can be no doubt (...)", Dames rightly observed, "that the [Washermen] caste described [by Barbosa] is the Veluthēdan or Vannāthan" (*ibid.*: 58, note 1). In the Madras Census Report, 1891, the Veluttēdan was defined "as the washerman of the Nāyars and higher castes in Malabar. He calls himself a Nāyar, and, in many cases, was returned as of that main caste"; "in the Travancore and Cochin Census Reports, 1901, Veluttētan and Veluthēdan are given respectively as an occupational title and sub-division of Nāyars" (Thurston and Rangachari 1909, vol. VII: 389). Moreover, "in the matter of food and drink, as also in their dress and ornaments, [the Veluthēdans] resemble the Nāyars" (*ibid.*: 391).

with them"; the Nayars, however, "may take their women as concubines" (*ibid.*: 58).

The Weavers, the Caletis in Barbosa's account,[3] did not mix with any other caste but a Nayar could take one of their women as his mistress. Many Weavers, therefore, were "sons of *Nayres* and fine men in their appearance"; they often exhibited their military proclivity and "carry arms and go to the wars where they fight well" (*ibid.*: 59). After indulging in sexual intercourse with a woman from one of these castes, a Nayar man would bathe and change his clothes before returning home.

IV

It was stated that all castes placed below the "honourable people" were of low status: "thence downwards there are also divers sects of low and base people who are all serfs of the king and other lords and governors of the country" (Barbosa [Stanley]1866: 116). Another separation, however, appears in the text: besides Potters, Washermen and Weavers, "there are eleven others lower than they with whom the others do not associate, nor do they touch them under pain of death" (Barbosa [Dames] 1921: 59). They had in common their duty of obedience to rules of distance pollution.

The Tuias (*Tīyyans*) were mentioned first. Each of the following castes was introduced by a formula that seemed to announce a new step on a downward scale: "there is another caste lower and ruder"; "even lower and baser"... The assertion

3. The Caletis (Chāliyans) are described by Barbosa as a "low caste folk (who) have but little money, so that they clothe the lower races" (*ibid.*: 59). According to Thurston and Rangachari, the word "Chāliyan [sometimes] occurs as an occupational title or sub-division of Nāyars" (1909, vol. II: 14).

that a given caste is "still lower" than the preceding one does not illuminate the nature of their relationship. Barbosa alluded to the "great difference and separation" between the eleven castes in question but even *tiny differences* could justify *radical separations*: although the Mogeres (Mukayars) were declared "almost the same as the *Tuias*, (…) they do not touch one another" (*ibid.*: 64).[4] How could one define the supposed "similarity" of these two groups, and why should the Mogeres, generally mentioned after the Tuias, be considered "lower" than them?

Tuias	**Mogeres**
"Their work is mainly that of tending the palm-groves, and gathering the fruit thereof, and carrying it away for wages on their backs, for there are no beasts of burden in the land" (*ibid.*: 60).	"The most of them gain their living on the sea, they are sailors, and some of them fishers. (…) Some are very rich and own the ships in which they sail and trade with the Moors" (*ibid.*: 64).

Barbosa had no way of constructing a scale based on criteria common to the castes in question: some were very rich, but others were very poor; some dwelled in "huts very strait and mean", built "in secret lurking places whither folk of good caste never go save by mischance" (*ibid.*: 68); others had "large houses and farms, of which the King takes possession whensoever he will" (*ibid.*: 65). Some were sorcerers, "worse than devils" (*ibid.*: 69), while others were great astrologers whose skills were widely recognized by "honourable people".

Most versions mention the Manens (Mannans) *after* the Mogeres and the Canaquas (Kaniyans, Astrologers) *after* the Manens. Little information is given about the latter, who "are

4. Generally placed immediately after the Tuias, the Mogeres appear in fifth position in the version translated by Dames.

washermen for the common people" (*ibid.*: 61).[5] The Astrologers, on the other hand, are the subject of fairly detailed information: "Their trade is making bucklers and umbrellas; they learn letters for purposes of astronomy"; they foretell "with great truth things that are to come" (*ibid.*: 61-2). Their relations with the "respectable" castes are necessarily ambiguous even though they are quite frequent: "If the Kings would know what is to happen they summon these men, and going forth to their fruit gardens behind their palaces meet them there, and ask them whatsoever they desire to learn". Their reputation was such that no important decision could be taken without knowing their opinion: "No King or Lord will undertake any business, nor go forth from his house without asking them the day and the hour on which he shall do it" (*ibid.*: 62). Similarly, the greater merchants did not dare to undertake a business trip without previously consulting them.

Thurston and Rangachari reproduced Barbosa's testimony in full (Stanley 1866: 139) and added new details emphasizing the dignity of the Kaniyans, their talent and intellectual abilities: they "are easily recognized by their punctilious cleanness of person and clothing, the iron style and knife tucked into the waist, the palm umbrella with its ribs holding numbers of horoscopes (…). Most of them are intelligent, and well versed in Malayālam and Sanskrit" (1909, III: 186). The skills generally granted to them explain why they "are practically the guiding spirits in all the social and domestic concerns of Travancoreans, and even Muhammadans and Christians do not fail to profit by their wisdom":

---

5. The Mannans, also called Vannans are "a low class of Malabar washermen, who wash only for the polluting castes and for the higher castes when they are under pollution following births, deaths, etc..It is believed by the higher castes that such pollution can only be removed by wearing cloths washed by Mannáns, though at other times these cause pollution to them" (Francis, W. 1902: 167).

> *From the moment of the birth of an infant, which is noted by the Kaniyan for the purpose of casting its horoscope, to the moment of death, the services of the village astrologer are constantly in requisition. He is invariably consulted as to the cause of all calamities, and the cautious answers that he gives satisfy the people* (ibid.: 188).

Why was the status of the Kaniyans lower than that of the Mannans? Barbosa would not be able to explain it…

V

The notes accompanying Dames' translation – especially those relating to the Malabar kingdoms – were also an attempt at interpretation. This was in fact a "recreation", an abusive reconstruction of Barbosa's text.

By the time Dames published his translation, Risley's thesis was far from attracting unconditional approval. We saw that the tables of social precedence intended to legitimate his arguments proved impracticable. In the eyes of the provincial superintendents, British and Indian, the idea of a caste hierarchy derived from public opinion was a pure abstraction. But Dames thought he could confirm Risley's views based on his own interpretation of the *Book of Duarte Barbosa*. He did not hesitate to evoke "Barbosa's order of precedence" concerning the castes of Malabar. In his opinion, the traveller's list was quite accurate; although not exhaustive, it included "nearly all the castes of importance which still exist in Malabar (…)" (*ibid.*: 70, note 2). Dames also believed that there was order in this arrangement of castes. The principles behind this order were of course ignored, but this appeared secondary – except at the top of the status ladder, where "corrections" were necessary. And Dames "corrected" Barbosa, as we will now see.

We noted that the pre-eminence of Sovereignty, symbolized in Gujarat by the military elites, remained constant in the different contexts addressed by the author. Merchants and Brahmins (Gujarat) or Brahmins and Merchants (Vijayanagar, Calicut) complete the list of the "three functions". Relative arbitrariness also characterized the enumeration of the "honourable" castes of the Malabar even when it was stated that justice was exercised in accordance with social dignity.

Potters, Washermen and Weavers were not ordered in relation to each other any more than the "honourable people". With regard to the eleven Untouchable castes, ordering criteria were absent, as we have seen. Dames completely missed this fact. In the version of the account he translated, the Mogeres appear in *fifth* position, although they are declared "almost the same" as the Tuias, placed in the *first* position of the series. It is therefore the nature of Dames' arguments that we must examine.

In the preface to the second volume of his translation, he had admitted that the traveller's long familiarity with Malabar had made a faithful description of the caste system possible. However, a few pages later, he changed his mind:

> *The Brahmans, though strictly speaking the highest caste are here placed by Barbosa after the Kings or ruling families whom he no doubt considered to be entitled by their position to the first state, for to a European of that period it must have been unimaginable that a "King" should be of lower rank than a subject* (ibid.: 33, note 1).

In Dames' view, Barbosa's *faithful* description of the caste system had a crucial flaw: the traveller had attached too much importance to the King's role. Let us consider this aspect of his interpretation.

The question of the origin of the Rulers of Malabar had been reconsidered recently. Would it be possible to associate them with a particular caste? They seemed to be linked to the obscure identity of the Samantans, described by Dames as "an aristocracy above the ordinary Nāyars, but identical with them in their customs" (*ibid.*: 13, note 2). But it was not that simple. Thurston and Rangachari had gathered confusing information about them: Samantan, they wrote, is the name of "the caste of Malayālam Rājahs and chieftains". However, they also specified that it "is hardly a separate caste at all, at any rate at present, for those Nāyars and others who have at any time been petty chieftains in the country call them Sāmantas" (1909, Vol. VI: 280). Another passage alludes to Samantan Brahmins; and there was the testimony of someone who, after having "stated in court that he was 'a Sāmantan by caste', [clarified that] a Sāmantan is neither a Brāhman, nor a Kshatriya, nor a Vaisya, nor a Sūdra'" (*ibid.*: 281).

All this, of course, was totally ignored by the Portuguese traveller: the Kings of Malabar, he had declared from the outset, "are of one caste and custom" (*ibid.*: 6-7). But Dames' questions created a strange imbroglio as presented below in his own terms:

1. "The castes mentioned (…) by Barbosa amount actually to seventeen…

2. …but there is no doubt that he considers the Kings or Royal Sāmantans to be a separate caste, which is correct, as they were distinct from the Nāyars.

3. Including the Royal Caste and some Royal Sāmantans, among whom some are Kshatriyas, there are seven names in the first group, and eleven in the second, making a total of eighteen" (*ibid.*: 70, note 2).

The last statement makes it incomprehensible that Kings were excluded from what Dames claimed to be the list of castes "mentioned by Barbosa in the order he assigns to them":

1. Brahmins
2. Nayres
3. Biabares
4. Cuiavens
5. Mainatos
6. Çaletis + 11 "lower castes" = 17 castes

Table 25: *Barbosa's castes reconsidered* (according to Dames 1921: 71, note. 2).

Described as "Barbosa's order of precedence", this list is of course a re-elaboration – an illegitimate remake, in the spirit of Risley's thesis. For those who had accepted Risley's perspective, the supremacy of the Brahmins was indisputable. So Dames credited Barbosa with an idea of social precedence from which the Zamorin had been banished. The traveller had never expressed such a view.

Bernard Cohn ignored Barbosa's text, adopting Dames' fictional interpretation. Only in the light of this interpretation could he attribute to the Portuguese traveller the far-fetched role of a forerunner: "In many respects European accounts for the next 250 years do not progress much beyond Barbosa's reporting" (1990: 140). Like Dames, he assumed that the hierarchy of castes – postulated and introduced into the academic world at the beginning of the 20th century – had after all been immediately recognized and accurately described at the beginning of the 16th century.

C. G. Fuller endorses the same perspective: Barbosa had "anticipated by several centuries the results of modern anthropological research" (1976: 5). Most early European travellers, he writes, had mentioned a limited number of castes, without having grasped "the complexity of the hierarchical relations" (*ibid.*: 12). Barbosa had been an exception: "he refers to eighteen castes, if we include the royal lineages as one, ranging from the Brahmans to the Parayas)" (*ibid.*). In fact, Fuller *does not quote* Barbosa; he alludes instead to Dames' interpretation, although he has misread it. If, like Dames, one considers a sequence "ranging from the Brahmans to the Parayas", Kings and royal lineages have to be excluded, so only seventeen castes can be taken into account; if, like Barbosa, one considers eighteen castes, then Brahmins are not placed in the first position... Fuller merges both perspectives into an unexpected synthesis, departing simultaneously from Barbosa's account and Dames' "corrections".

***

Cohn had precise motivations. Dames' views offered him a means of strengthening his criticism of 18th century Orientalists. He harshly blamed the British scholar-administrators for having imagined that the texts of the Sanskrit tradition were "accurate guides to the culture and society of the Hindus" (1990: 142). Those texts suggested that the Brahmins were the dominant group in society – a perspective that, he noted, was refuted by the "political structure of the late eighteenth- and early nineteenth- century India" (*ibid.*: 143).

It is true that Barbosa did not depend on the Sanskrit tradition but, following Dames' fiction, Cohn assumed that he had attributed to the Brahmins exactly the same authority ascribed to them by the Orientalists.

According to Nicholas Dirks, colonial rule "made caste what it is today"; in his opinion, "it was under the British that 'caste' became a single term capable of expressing, organizing, and above all systematizing India's diverse forms of social identity, community, and organization" (2001: 5).

The Western perception of India would then have been transformed; texts written before the 18th century, the author argues, testifies to the reduced significance of caste: early foreign observers – both Europeans (like Barbosa) and non-Europeans (like Abu'l Fazl) had been quite discreet about this topic: caste "was barely mentioned" (*ibid.*: 19).

It is remarkable that, to highlight the difference in the Western perspective on India, *before* and *after* the 18th century, Cohn and Dirks support such radically opposed ideas. While the former believed that Barbosa had collected valuable information about the caste system, the latter states that he had been rather laconic in this regard: "although he reported the position of Brahmans as exalted and that of the untouchables as inferior, he did not mention the varna system (…) nor did he moralize about caste one way or the other" (*ibid.*).

It is not true that Barbosa skirted the caste issue: he was quite aware of the multiplicity of groups, referred to extensively in the section of his book on the kingdoms of Malabar. But Barbosa's alleged silence is indispensable to Dirks' thesis, whose arguments must be recalled. In the eyes of the early European travellers,

1. caste "did not seem particularly striking, important or fixed";

2. "this was [partly due to the fact that] the European world was itself mired in hierarchical forms" (*ibid.*: 20).

This is a problematic argument. Barbosa – like other European travellers of the time – had recognized castes in India without according them too much importance since his society was "itself mired in hierarchical forms". Caste and hierarchy are therefore assimilated, as if the reality of the former necessarily presupposed that of the latter.

Dames noted that the tripartite division of the Hindu population of Vijayanagar was inspired by the ancient European theory of the three "states". But what can one conclude from this? As strongly emphasized by Georges Duby, the medieval theory of the three social functions was "a framework for an ideal classification" (1980: 6) but never mirrored a *social* hierarchy. It was an "axiomatic truth, whose existence is never proved, never evoked but in relation to a cosmology, a theology, and certainly a morality" (*ibid.*: 8).

A Portuguese text written around 1438 expresses the conceptual autonomy of the ternary structure in a universe characterized by the proliferation of new professions and social classes.[6] Although five "states" were now mentioned, the discontinuity between the first three and the last two is unequivocal. The elements of the canonical triad are immediately recognized: (1) "oradores" (*oratores*); (2) "defenssores" (*bellatores*); (3) "lavradores e pescadores" (*farmers and fishermen,* instead of *laboratores*). The third "state" is referred to as the foundation of the entire construction: "the feet" that hold and support all public affairs (*os pees em que toda a cousa publica se mantem e soporta*). The plethora of new professions was spread over two new "states", neither of them endowed with visible internal coherence. They included physicians, surgeons, sailors, musicians, gunsmiths, goldsmiths and many others who, it was noted, do not even deserve to be named – there were "such a large number of trades that it is not possible to take account of them". No hierarchical scheme had been planned.

Dirks assumes however a well-structured European hierarchy – which he believes had prevailed in 16th century Europe and was analogous to the Hindu social system. This explained, in his view, why Barbosa considered unnecessary to talk... about castes. This argument does not essentially differ from Cohn's premise. In the authors' descriptions, the concept of caste hierarchy does not apply to reality, being no more than the imaginary support of a historical construction.

6. Roquete 1842.

BIBLIOGRAPHY

Agassiz, Louis

1962 (1859). *Essay on Classification*. Cambridge (Massachusetts).

Aiyar, Subramhanya N.

1903: *Census of India, 1901. Travancore*. Part I. Report. Trivandrum.

Allen, N. J.

1985: "Hierarchical Opposition and some Other Types of Relation" in Barnes, R. H. *et al.* (eds.): 21-32.

Anstey, Vera

1936 (1929): *The Economic Development of India*. London.

App, Urs.

2010: *The Birth of Orientalism*. Philadelphia.

Appadurai, Arjun

1986: "Is Homo Hierarchicus?", in *American Ethnologist*, 13 (4) 745-761.

1988: "Putting hierarchy in its place", in *Cultural Anthropology*, 3 (1): 36-49

1993: "Number in the Colonial Imagination", in Breckenridge, Carol A. and Peter van der Veer (eds.): 314-339.

Apthorpe, Raymond

1984: "Hierarchy and Other Social Relations: Some Categorial Logic", in Galey, Jean-Claude (ed.): 283-298.

Arnold, David

1988: *Famine. Social Crisis and Historical Change*. Oxford.

1999: "Hunger in the Garden of Plenty: The Bengal Famine of 1770", in Johns, Alessa (ed.): 81-111.

Ascoli, F. D.

1917: *Early Revenue History of Bengal and the Fifth Report, 1812*. Oxford.

Aspinall, A.

1931: *Cornwallis in Bengal*. Manchester.

Babb, Lawrence

1975: *The Divine Hierarchy: Popular Hinduism in Central India.* New York.

Baden-Powell, B. H.

1892: *The Land-Systems of British India*. Oxford. 3 vols.

1899: *The Origin and Growth of Village Communities in India.* London.

Bailey, F. G.

1957: *Caste and the Economic Frontier. A Village in Highland Orissa.* Manchester.

1960: *Tribe, Caste, and Nation. A Study of Political Activity and Political Change in Highland Orissa.* Manchester.

Baines, J. A.

1893: *General Report on the Census of India, 1891.* London.

1912: *Ethnography. Castes and Tribes.* Strassburg.

Bannerman, A. D.

1902: *Census of India 1901. Rajputana.* Part I. Report. Lucknow.

Barbosa, Duarte

1866: *A Description of the Coasts of East Africa and Malabar in the beginning of the Sixteenth Century*. Translated from an early Spanish manuscript in the Barcelona Library with notes and a Preface by Henry E. J. Stanley. London.

1918: *The Book of Duarte Barbosa. An Account of the Countries Bordering on the Indian Ocean and their Inhabitants, written by Duarte Barbosa, and completed about the Year 1518 A. D.* Vol. I, including the Coasts of East Africa, Arabia, Persia, and Western India as far as the Kingdom of Vijayanagar. Translated and annotated by M. L. Dames. London.

1921: *The Book of Duarte Barbosa. An Account of the Countries Bordering on the Indian Ocean and their Inhabitants, written by Duarte Barbosa, and completed about the Year 1518 A. D.* Vol. II, including the Coasts of Malabar, Eastern India, Further India, China and the Indian Archipelago. Translated and annotated by M. L. Dames. London.

1996: *O Livro de Duarte Barbosa.* Vol. I: Introdução, Texto Crítico e Apêndice por Maria Augusta da Veiga e Sousa. Lisboa.

2000: *O Livro de Duarte Barbosa.* Vol. II: Prefácio, Texto Crítico e Apêndice por Maria Augusta da Veiga e Sousa. Lisboa.

Barnes, R. H.

1985: "Hierarchy without Caste", in Barnes, R. H. *et al.* (eds.): 8-20.

Barnes, R. H., Daniel de Coppet and R. J. Parkin (eds.)

1985: *Contexts and Levels. Anthropological Essays on Hierarchy*. Oxford.

Barrier, N. Gerald (ed.)

1981: *The Census in British India. New Perspectives.* Delhi.

Bates, Crispin

1995: "Race, Caste and Tribe in Central India: The Early Origins of Indian Anthropometry", in Robb, Peter (ed.): 165-218.

Bayly, Susan

1995: "Caste and 'Race' in the Colonial Ethnography of India, in Robb, Peter (ed.): 165-218.

1999: *Caste, Society and Politics in India, from the Eighteenth Century to the Modern Age.* Cambridge.

Bentham, Jeremy

1907 (1789): *An Introduction to the Principles of Morals and Legislation.* Oxford.

Bernier, François

1916 (1671): *Travels in the Mogul Empire AD 1656-1668.* Translated and annotated by Archibald Constable. Oxford.

Berreman, Gerald D.

1965: "The Study of Caste Ranking in India", in *Southwestern Journal of Anthropology*, 21 (2): 115-29.

Béteille, André

1977: *Inequality Among Men*. Oxford.

1987: *The Idea of Natural Inequality an Other Essays*. Delhi.

1991: *Society and Politics in India: Essays in a Comparative Perspective*. London.

1996: "Varna and jati", in *Sociological Bulletin*, 45, 1: 15-27.

Beverley, H.

1872: *Report on the Census of Bengal, 1872*. Calcutta.

Bhagat, Ram B.

2006: "Census and Caste enumeration: British Legacy and Contemporary Practice in India", in *Genus*, 62, 2: 119-134.

Bhattacharya, Jogendra Nath

1896: *Hindu Castes and Sects*. Calcutta.

Bhattacharyya-Panda, Nandini

2008: *Appropriation and Invention of Tradition. The East India Company and Hindu Law in Early Colonial Bengal*. Oxford.

Biardeau, Madeleine

1971-72: "Brahmanes et Potiers", in *Annuaire de l'École Pratique des Hautes Études, 5ème Section, Sciences Religieuses*: 31-55.

Blackstone, William

1765: *Commentaries on the Laws of England.* Vol. I. Oxford.

Blunt, E. A. H.

1912: *United Provinces of Agra and Oudh (Census of India, 1911)*. Part I. Report. Allahabad.

1931: *The Caste System of Northern India with special Reference to the United Provinces of Agra and Oudh.* London.

Bouglé, Célestin

1899: *Les Idées égalitaires*. Paris.

1900: "Remarques sur le régime des castes", in *Année Sociologique*, IV: 1-64.

1907 a: *Le Solidarisme*. Paris.

1907 b: *Qu'est-ce que la sociologie?* Paris.

1969 [1908]: *Essais sur le régime des castes*. Paris.

1971: *Essays on the Caste System.* Translated with an introduction by D. F. Pocock. Cambridge.

Bouillier, V. et G. Toffin (eds.)

1993: *Classer les Dieux? Des Panthéons en Asie du Sud.* Paris

Bourdillon, J. A.

1883: *Report on the Census of Bengal, 1881.* Vol. I. Calcutta.

Bourke, John G.

1891: *Scatologic Rites of all Nations.* Washington.

Breckenridge, Carol A. and Peter van der Veer (eds.)

1993: *Orientalism and the Postcolonial Predicament. Perspectives on South India.* Philadelphia.

Brubaker, R. L.

1979: "Barbers, Washermen, and Other Priests; Servants of the South Indian Village and its Goddess", in *History of Religions*, 19: 128-152.

Buchanan, Francis

1807: *A Journey from Madras Through the Countries of Mysore, Canara and Malabar.* London. 3 vols.

Buffier, Claude

1726: *Traité de la société civile*. Paris.

Burghart, Richard

1978: "Hierarchical Models of the Hindu Social System", in *Man*, 13, 4: 519-36.

Burn, R.

1902: *Census of India 1901. N.-W. Provinces and Oudh.* Part I. Report. Allahabad.

Campbell, George

1852: *Modern India. A Sketch of the System of Civil Government*. London.

1876: "The Tenure of Land in India", in Probyn, J. W. (ed.): *Systems of Land Tenure in Various Countries*, London: 125-196.

1863: *Census of England and Wales for the year 1861*. General Report. Volume III. London.

Christian, G. J.

1854: *Report on the Census of the North West Provinces of the Bengal Presidency, taken on the 1st of January, 1853.* Calcutta.

Clark, J. C. D.

2000: *English Society 1660-1832: Religion, Ideology and Politics during the Ancien Régime.* Cambridge.

Clarke, G. E.

1985: "Hierarchy, Status and Social History in Nepal" in Barnes, R. H. *et al.* (eds.): 193-209.

Cohn, Bernard S.

1968: "Notes on the History of the Study of Indian Society and Culture". Reprinted in Cohn 1990: 136-71.

1990: *An Anthropologist Among the Historians and Other Essays*. Delhi.

1996: *Colonialism and its Forms of Knowledge. The British in India.* Princeton.

Colebrooke, Henry Thomas

1799: "Enumeration of Indian Classes", in *Asiatic Researches or Transactions of the Society Instituted in Bengal, for Inquiring into the History and Antiquities, the Arts, Sciences, and Literature of Asia,* 5: 53-67.

1804: *Remarks on the Husbandry and Internal Commerce of Bengal*. London.

Cornish, W. R.

1874: *Report on the Census of the Madras Presidency, 1871.* Vol. I. Madras.

Crooke, W.

1896: *The Tribes and Castes of the North-Western Provinces and Oudh*. Calcutta. 4 vols.

Dalton, Edward Tuite

1872: *Descriptive Ethnology of Bengal*. Calcutta.

Darwin, Charles

1859: *On the Origin of Species*. London.

Das, Veena

1977: *Structure and Cognition. Aspects of Hindu Caste and Ritual*. Delhi.

Davies, A. Mervyn

1935: *Strange Destiny. A Biography of Warren Hastings*. New York.

Deliège, Robert

1999: *The Untouchables of India*. Oxford.

Dew, Nicholas

2009: *Orientalism in Louis XIV's France*. Oxford.

Dirks, Nicholas B.

1987: *The Hollow Crown: Ethnohistory of an Indian Kingdom*. Cambridge.

1990: "The Original Caste: Power, History and Hierarchy in South Asia", in Marriott, McKim (ed.): *India through Hindu Categories*: 59-77.

2001: *Castes of Mind. Colonialism and the Making of Modern India*. Princeton.

2006: *The Scandal of Empire. India and the Creation of Imperial Britain*. Cambridge.

Dirks, Nicholas B. (ed.)

1992: *Colonialism and Culture*. Ann Arbor.

Doniger, Wendy

1980: *Women, Androgynes and Other Mythical Beasts*. Chicago.

Douglas, Mary

1966: *Purity and Danger. An Analysis of the Concept of Pollution and Taboo.* London.

Dow, Alexander

1768: *The History of Hindostan from the Earliest Account of Time to the Death of Akbar, translated from the Persian of Mahummud Casim Ferishtah of Delhi.* London. 2 vols.

1772: *The History of Hindostan from the Death of Akbar, to the Complete Settlement of the Empire under Aurungzeb to which are prefixed I. A Dissertation on the Origin and Nature of Despotism in Hindostan. II. An Enquiry into the State of Bengal; With a Plan for Restoring that Kingdom to its former Prosperity and Splendor.* London.

Driver, Peshotan Nasserwanji

1949: *Problems of Zamindari and Land Tenure Reconstruction in India.* Bombay.

Dube., S. C.

1955: *Indian Village.* London.

Dubois, Abbé J. A.

1906 (1897): *Hindu Manners, Customs and Ceremonies.* Translated from the author's late French ms. and edited with notes, corrections and biography by Henry K. Beauchamp. Oxford.

Duby, Georges

1978: *Les trois ordres ou l'imaginaire du féodalisme.* Paris.

1980: *The Three Orders. Feudal Society Imagined.* Translated by Arthur Goldhammer. Chicago.

Dumézil, Georges

1948: *Mitra-VaruGa. Essai sur deux représentations indo-européennes de la souveraineté.* Paris.

1968: *Mythe et épopée, I. L'idéologie des trois fonctions dans les épopées des peuples Indo-Européens.* Paris.

1988: *Mitra-Varuna. An Essay on Two Indo-European*

Representations of Sovereignty. Translated by Derek Coltman. New York.

Dumont, Louis

1957: *Une Sous-caste de l'Inde du Sud. Organisation sociale et religion des Pramalai Kallar*. Paris.

1966: *Homo hierarchicus. Essai sur le système des castes*. Paris.

1969: "Preface" to the 4th edition of Célestin Bouglé: *Essais sur le régime des castes*. Paris.

1975 (1964): *La Civilisation Indienne et nous*. Paris.

1977 a: *Homo Aequalis. Genèse et épanouissement de l'idéologie économique.* Paris.

1977 b: *From Mandeville to Marx: The Genesis and Triumph of Economic Ideology*. Chicago.

1979: "Postface", in *Homo hierarchicus. Le Système des castes et ses implications.* (Édition "Tel"). Paris.

1980: *Homo Hierarchicus. The Caste System and its Implications*. Translated by Mark Sainsbury, Louis Dumont, and Basia Gulati (2nd English edition). Chicago.

1982: "On Value" in *Proceedings of the British Academy*, 66: 207-41.

1986: *Essays on Individualism: Modern Ideology in Anthropological Perspective*. Chicago.

Durkheim, Emile

1893: *De la division du travail social*. Paris.

1933: *The Division of Labor in Society*. Translated by George Simpson. New York.

Dutt, N. K.

1931: *Origin and Growth of Caste in India.* Vol. I. Calcutta.

Ehrard, Jean

1994 (1963): *L'idée de nature en France dans la première moitié du XVIIIe siècle*. Paris.

Elmore, Wilber Theodore

1915: *Dravidian Gods in Modern Hinduism. A Study of the Local and Village Deities of Southern India.* New York.

Elwin, Verrier

1964: *The Tribal World of Verrier Elwin. An Autobiography.* Oxford.

Embree, Ainslie Thomas

1962: *Charles Grant and British Rule in India.* New York.

Enthoven, R. E.

1902: *Census of India, 1901. Bombay.* Part I. Report. Bombay.

Eyler, John M.

1979: *Victorian Social Medicine. The Ideas and Methods of William Farr*. Baltimore.

Farr, W.

1863: "The New Classification of the People according to their Employments", in *Census of England and Wales for the year 1861.* Vol. III. General Report: 225-232.

Fawcett, F.

1915 (1901): *Nâyars of Malabar*. Madras.

Feiling, Keith

1954: *Warren Hastings*. London.

Firminger, Walter Kelly

1917: *The Fifth Report from the Select Committee of the House of Commons on the Affairs of the East India Company.* Calcutta. 3 vols.

Foucault, Michel

1970: *The Order of Things: An Archaeology of the Human Sciences*. New York.

Francis, Philip

1782: *Original Minutes of the Governor-General and Council of Fort William on the Settlement and Collection of the Revenues of Bengal: with a Plan of Settlement, recommended to the Court of Directors in January, 1776.* London.

Francis, W.

1902: *Census of India, 1901. Madras.* Part I. Report. Madras.

Freed, Stanley A.

1963: "An Objective Method for Determining the Collective Caste Hierarchy of an Indian Village", in *American Anthropologist*, 65: 879-891.

Fryer, John

1909: *A New Account of East India and Persia being Nine Years' Travels, 1672-1681*. Vol. I. London.

Fuchs, Stephen

1950: *The Children of Hari. A Study of the Nimar Balahis in the Central Provinces of India*. Vienna.

Fuller, C. J.

1976: *The Nayars Today*. Cambridge.

1992: *The Camphor Flame. Popular Hinduism and Society in India.* Princeton.

2016: "Anthropologists and Viceroys: Colonial Knowledge and Policy Making in India, 1871-1912", in *Modern Asian Studies*, 50: 217-58.

2017: "Ethnographic Inquiry in Colonial India: Herbert Risley, William Crooke, and the Study of Tribes and Castes", in *Journal of the Royal Anthropological Institute*, 23 (3): 603-21.

2024: *Anthropologist and Imperialist. H. H. Risley and British India, 1873-1911*. London.

Gait, E. A.

1892: *Census of India, 1891. Assam.* Report. Vol. 1. Shillong.

1902: *Census of India, 1901. The Lower Provinces of Bengal and their Feudatories.* Part I. The Report. Calcutta.

1913: *Report on the Census of India 1911.* Part I. Vol. 1. Calcutta.

Galey, Jean-Claude (ed.)

1984: *Différences, valeurs, hiérarchies: Textes offerts à Louis Dumont*. Paris.

Gellner, David N. and Declan Quigley (eds.)

1999: *Contested Hierarchies. A Collaborative Ethnography of Caste Among the Newars of the Kathmandu Valley, Nepal*. Delhi.

Ghurye, G. S.

1932: *Caste and Race in India*. London.

1950: *Caste and Class in India*. Bombay.

Gomes da Silva, José Carlos

1989: *L'Identité volée. Essais d'anthropologie sociale*. Bruxelles.

2003: *O Discurso contra si próprio*. Lisboa.

2010: *The Cult of Jagannātha. Myths and Rituals*. Delhi.

2019: *Kṛṣṇa-Jagannātha in the Western Mind*. Delhi.

Gough, E. Kathleen

1959: "Criteria of Caste Ranking in South India", in *Man in India,* 39 (2): 115-26.

1960: "Caste in a Tanjore Village", in Leach, E. R. (ed.): 11-60.

Grant, Charles

1797: *Observations on the State of Society Among the Asiatic Subjects of Great-Britain, particularly with respect to morals; and on the means of improving it, written chiefly in the year 1792*.

Growse, F. S.

1882: *Mathurá: A District Memoir*. Delhi.

Guha, Ranajit

1996 (1963): *A Rule of Property for Bengal. An Essay on the Idea of Permanent Settlement*. Durham.

Guha, Sumit

2013: *Beyond Caste. Identity and Power in South Asia, Past and Present.* Leiden.

Guigue, Bruno

2004: "Montesquieu ou les paradoxes du relativisme", in *Études*, 401: 193-204.

Gupta, Dipankar

2000: *Interrogating Caste. Understanding Hierarchy and Difference in Indian Society.* Delhi.

Haara, Heikki

2018: *Pufendorf's Theory of Sociability: Passions, Habits and Social Order.* Cham.

Halbfass, Wilhelm

1988: *India and Europe. An Essay in Understanding*. Albany.

Hamilton, Richard F.

1996: *The Social Misconstruction of Reality. Validity and Verification in the Scholarly Community.* New Haven.

Hamilton, Walter

1820: *A Geographical, Statistical, and Historical Description of Hindostan, and the Adjacent Countries*. London. 2 vols.

Hastings, Warren

1785: "Introduction" to *Bhăgvăt-Gēētā, or Dialogues of Krěěshnă and Ărjŏŏn in Eighteen Lectures, with Notes*. Translated by Charles Wilkins. London.

Heck, Christian

1997: *L'Échelle céleste dans l'art du Moyen-Âge. Une histoire de la quête du ciel.* Paris.

Heesterman, J. C.

1985: *The Inner Conflict of Tradition. Essays in Indian Ritual, Kingship, and Society*. Chicago.

1993: *The Broken World of Sacrifice: An Essay in Ancient Indian Ritual*. Chicago.

Herrenschmidt, Olivier

1989: *Les Meilleurs dieux sont hindous*. Lausanne.

Hiltebeitel, Alf

1980: "Rāma and Gilgamesh: The Sacrifices of the Water Buffalo and the Bull of Heaven", in *History of Religions*, 19, 3: 187-223.

1988: *The Cult of Draupadī. Mythologies: From Gingee to Kurukcetra.* Chicago.

1991: *The Cult of Draupadī. On Hindu Ritual and the Goddess.* Chicago.

2011: *Dharma. Its Early History in Law, Religion, and Narrative*. Oxford.

Hiltebeitel, Alf (ed.)

1989: *Criminal Gods and Demon Devotees. Essays on the Guardians of Popular Hinduism*. New York.

Hobbes, Thomas

1900 [1651]: *Leviathan or The Matter, Forme and Power of a Commonwealth Ecclesiasticall and Civil*. Cambridge.

Hocart, A. M.

1938: *Les Castes*. Paris.

1950: *Caste. A Comparative Study*. London.

Hofstadter, Douglas

1979: *Gödel, Escher, Bach: An Eternal Golden Braid*. New York.

Holwell, John Zephaniah

1765-1771: *Interesting Historical Events, relative to the Provinces of Bengal, and the Empire of Indostan*. London. 3 vols.

Houseman, Michael

1984: "La relation hiérarchique: idéologie particulière ou modèle général?", in Galey, Jean-Claude (ed.): 299-318.

Howell, Signe

1985: "Equality and Hierarchy in Chewong Classification", in Barnes, R. H. *et al.* (eds.): 167-80.

Howes, Jennifer

2010: *Illustrating India. The Early Colonial Investigations of Colin Mackenzie (1784-1821)*. Delhi.

Hume, David

1742: "Of the Rise and Progress of the Arts and Sciences", in *Essays: Moral, Political, and Literary*, Vol. I: 174-197.

1889 (1777): *Essays, Moral, Political and Literary*. Vol. I. London.

Hunter, W. W.

1868: *The Annals of Rural Bengal*. Vol. I. London.

1875: *A Statistical Account of Bengal*. Vol. I. London.

1886: *The Indian Empire. Its History, People, and Products.* London.

Hutton, J. H.

1933: *Census of India, 1931.* Part I. Report. Vol. I. Delhi.

1946: *Caste in India. Its Nature, Function, and Origins.* Cambridge.

Ibbetson, Denzil

1916 (1883): *Panjab Castes*. Lahore.

Inden, Ronald

1990: *Imagining India*. Oxford.

Irving, B. A.

1853: *The Theory and Practice of Caste; being an Inquiry into the Effects of Caste on the Institutions and Probable Destinies of the Anglo-Indian Empire*. London.

Jacquemont, Victor.

1841: *Voyage dans l'Inde pendant les années 1828 à 1832.* Vol. I. Paris.

Jamison, Stephanie W.

1996: *Sacrificed Wife / Sacrificer's Wife. Women, Ritual, and Hospitality in Ancient India*. New York.

Johns, Alessa (ed.)

1999: *Dreadful Visitations. Confronting Natural Catastrophe in the Age of Enlightenment*. New York.

Jones, William

1807: *The Works of Sir William Jones*. London. 13 vols.

Kejariwal, O. P.

1988: *The Asiatic Society of Bengal and the Discovery of India's Past: 1784-1838*. Delhi.

Ketkar, Shridar V.

1909: *The History of Caste in India.* Vol. I. Ithaca, N. Y.

Khare, R. S.

1984: *The Untouchable as Himself: Ideology, Identity, and Pragmatism among the Lucknow Chamars*. Cambridge.

Khare, R. S. (ed.)

2006: *Caste, Hierarchy, and Individualism. Indian Critiques of Louis Dumont's Contributions*. Oxford.

Kieffer, J.-L.

1983: *Anquetil-Duperron. L'Inde en France au XVIIIe siècle*. Paris.

Kitts, Eustace J.

1885: *A Compendium of the Castes and Tribes found in India: compiled from the (1881) Census Reports for the various Provinces, (excluding Burmah) and Native States of the Empire*. Bombay.

Kolenda, Pauline M.

1981: *Caste, Cult and Hierarchy. Essays on Culture of India*. Meerut.

Konale, S. B. and H. K. Bhat

2007: "Religion and Society among the Coorgs of South India: Some Conceptual and Methodological Issues", in Misra, P. K. *et al.* (eds.): 113-128.

Kopf, David

1969: *British Orientalism and the Bengal Renaissance. The Dynamics of Indian Modernization: 1773-1835*. Berkeley.

Lardinois, Roland

2007: *L'invention de l'Inde. Entre ésorérisme et science*. Paris.

Laval-Reviglio, Marie-Claire

1987: "Les conceptions politiques des Physiocrates", in *Revue Française de Science Politique*: 181-213.

Le Goff, Jacques

1979: "Les trois fonctions indo-europeennes, l'historien et l'Europe féodale", in *Annales. Économies. Sociétés. Civilisations*, 34e année, n°. 6: 1187-1215.

1985: *L'Imaginaire médiéval*. Paris.

1988: *The Medieval Imagination*. Translated by Arthur Goldhammer. Chicago.

Leach, Edmund E. R. (ed.)

1960: *Aspects of Caste in South India, Ceylon and North-West Pakistan.* Cambridge.

Lemercier de la Rivière, Pierre-Paul

1767: *L'Ordre naturel et essentiel des sociétés politiques*. London.

Lévi, Sylvain

1905: *Le Népal. Étude historique d'un Royaume Hindou.* Vol. I. Paris.

Lincoln, Bruce

1999: *Theorizing Myth. Narrative, Ideology, and Scholarship.* Chicago.

Linnaeus, Carolus

1964: *Systema Naturae 1735. Facsimile of the first edition.* Nieuwkoop.

Locke, John.

1821 [1689-90]: *Two Treatises of Government*. London.

Lord, Henry

1999 (1630): *A Display of Two Forraigne Sects in the East Indies.* London.

Lorenzen, David N.

2006: *Who Invented Hinduism? Essays on Religion and History.* New Delhi.

Lovejoy, Arthur O.

1964 (1936): *The Great Chain of Being. A Study of the History of an Idea.* Cambridge, Massachusetts.

Lyall, Alfred C.

1882: *Asiatic Studies, Religious and Social.* Vol. I. London.

Lynch, Owen M.

1969: *The Politics of Untouchability*. New York.

Madan, T. N. (ed.)

1982: *Way of Life. King, Householder, Renouncer. Essays in Honour of Louis Dumont.* Delhi.

Magrath, C.F.

1872: "Memorandum on the Tribes and Castes of the Province of Behar", in Beverley, H.: 155-179.

Mahar, J. Michael (ed.)

1972: *The Untouchables in Contemporary India.* Tucson.

Mahar, Pauline M.

1959: "A Multiple Scaling Technique for Caste Ranking", in *Man in India*, 39 (2): 127-47.

Malamoud, Charles

1989: *Cuire le monde. Rite et pensée dans l'Inde Ancienne.* Paris.

1996: *Cooking the World, Ritual and Thought in Ancient India.* Translated by David White. Delhi.

Mallory, J. P.

1989: *In Search of the Indo-Europeans. Language, Archaeology and Myth.* London.

Manu

1886: *The Laws of Manu.* Translated by G. Bühler. The Sacred Books of the East, XXV. Oxford.

Marglin, Frédérique Apffel

1985: *Wives of the God-King. The Rituals of the Devadasis of Puri.* Delhi.

Marriott, McKim

1960 [1955]: "Social Structure and Change in a U. P. Village", in Srinivas, M. (ed.): 106-121.

1960 [1958]: *Caste Ranking and Community Structure in Five Regions of India and Pakistan.* Poona.

1968: "Caste Ranking and Food Transactions: A Matrix Analysis", in Singer, Milton and Bernard S. Cohn (eds.): 133-171.

Marriott, McKim (ed.)

1955: *Village India. Studies in the Little Community*. Chicago.

1990: *India Through Hindu Categories*. Delhi.

Marshall, P. J.

1970: *The British Discovery of Hinduism in the Eighteenth Century.* Cambridge.

Marten, J. T.

1924: *Census of India, 1921.* Part I. Report. Calcutta.

Masilamani-Meyer, Eveline

1989: "The Changing Face of Kāttavarāyan", in Hiltebeitel, Alf (ed.): 69-103.

2004: *Kāttavarāyal Katai. The Story of Kāttavarāyal.* An Annotated Translation. Wiesbaden.

Max Müller, Friedrich

1847: "On the relation of the Bengali to the Aryan and Aboriginal Languages in India", in *Report of the British Association for the Advancement of Science:* 319-350.

Mayer, Adrian C.

1956: "Some Hierarchical Aspects of Caste", in *Southwestern Journal of Anthropology*, 12: 117-44.

1960: *Caste and Kinship in Central India. A Village and its Region.* London.

Metcalf, Thomas R.

1995: *Ideologies of the Raj*. Cambridge.

Mill, James

1817: *The History of British India*. Vol. I. London.

1820: "Government" (*Supplement to the Encyclopaedia Britannica).* Reprinted in Mill, James, 1825: 3-32.

1825: *Essays on Government, Jurisprudence, Liberty of the Press, and Law of Nations*. London.

Misra, P. K., K. K. Basa and H. K. Bhat (eds.)

2007: *M. N. Srinivas. The Man and His Work.* Jaipur.

Moffatt, Michael

1979: *An Untouchable Community in South India. Structure and Consensus.* Princeton.

Montesquieu, Charles-Louis de Secondat

1748: *De L'Esprit des Loix.* Genève. 2 vols.

1899-1900: *The Spirit of Laws.* Translated from the French by Thomas Nugent. New York. 2 vols.

Mukherjee, S. N.

1968: *Sir William Jones. A Study in the Eighteenth-Century British Attitudes to India.* Cambridge.

Murr, Sylvia

1983: "Les conditions d'émergence du discours sur l'Inde au siècle des Lumières", in *Puruṣārtha*, 7: 233-84.

1987 a: *L'Inde philosophique entre Bossuet et Voltaire. I: Moeurs et coutumes des Indiens (1777). Un inédit du Père G.-L. Coeurdoux s.j. dans la version de N.-J. Desvaulx.* Paris.

1987 b: *L'Inde philosophique entre Bossuet et Voltaire. II: L'Indologie du Père Coeurdoux. Stratégies, apologétique et scientificité.* Paris.

Nandy, Ashis

1983: *The Intimate Enemy. Loss and Recovery of Self Under Colonialism.* Delhi.

Nelson, James Henry

1868: *The Madura country. A Manual.* Madras.

Nesfield, John Collinson

1885: *Brief View of the Caste System of the North-Western Provinces and Oudh.* Allahabad.

O'Donnell, C. J.

1893: *Census of India, 1891. The Lower Provinces of Bengal and Their Feudatories.* The Report. Vol. III. Calcutta.

O'Malley, L. S. S.

1913: *Census of India, 1911. Bengal, Bihar and Orissa and*

Sikkim. Part I. Report. Calcutta.

1932: *Indian Caste Customs*. Cambridge.

Parkin, Robert

2002: *Louis Dumont and Hierarchical Opposition*. New York.

Parry, Jonathan P.

1979: *Caste and Kinship in Kangra*. London.

1980: "Ghosts, Greed and Sin: The Occupational Identity of the Benares Funeral Priests", in *Man*, 15 (1): 88-111.

1994: *Death in Benares*. Cambridge.

Paterson, J. D.

1808: "Of the Origin of the Hindu Religion", in *Asiatic Researches*, 8: 44-87.

Pattullo, Henry

1772: *An Essay upon the Cultivation of the Lands, and Improvements of the Revenues of Bengal*. London.

Pennington, Brian K.

2005: *Was Hinduism Invented? Britons, Indians, and the Colonial Construction of Religion.* Oxford.

Plowden, William Chichele

1867: *Census of the N.W. Provinces, 1865.* Vol. I. General Report. Allahabad.

1873: *Census of the N.W. Provinces, 1872.* Vol. I. General Report, and Statements and Tables. Allahabad.

1883: *Report on the Census of India taken on 17th February 1881.* London.

Prinsep, James

1832: "Census of the Population of the City of Benares", in *Asiatic Researches*, 17: 470-98.

Probyn, J. W. (ed.)

1876: *Systems of Land Tenure in Various Countries*. London.

Pufendorf, Samuel

1719 (1695): *An Introduction to the History of the Principal*

Kingdoms and States of Europe. Translated by Jodocus Crull. London.

1729 (1672): *Of the Law of Nature and Nations.* Translated by Basil Kennett from the original, "De jure naturae et gentium". London.

Quesnay, François

1765: "Observations sur le droit naturel des hommes réunis en société" in Theré, Christine *et al.* (eds.). Vol. 1: 97-109.

1766: "Remarques sur l'opinion de l'auteur de l'*Esprit des loix* concernant les colonies" in Theré, Christine *et al.* (eds.). Vol. 2: 869-79.

1767 a: "Maximes générales du gouvernement économique d'un royaume agricole", in Theré, Christine *et al.* (eds.). Vol. 1: 565-96.

1767 b: "Despotisme de la Chine", in Theré, Christine *et al.* (eds.). Vol. 2: 1005-114.

Quigley, Declan

1993: *The Interpretation of Caste*. Oxford.

Raheja, Gloria Goodwin

1988: *The Poison in the Gift. Ritual, Prestation, and the Dominant Caste in a North Indian Village.* Chicago.

Ramanujan, A. K.

1990: "Is There an Indian Way of Thinking?", in Marriott, McKim (ed.): 41-58.

Ramsay, A. M.

1722: *Essai philosophique sur le gouvernement civil*. London.

Ranade, Mahadev Govind

1906 (1898): *Essays on Indian Economics*. Madras.

Rauschenbusch-Clough, Emma

1899: *While Sewing Sandals or Tales of a Telugu Pariah Tribe*. London.

Raynal, G.-Th.

1770: *Histoire philosophique et politique des établissements &*

du commerce des Européens dans les deux Indes. Amsterdam. 4 vols.

1866: *Report on the Census of Calcutta for the year 1866*. Calcutta.

Rio, K. M. and O. H. Smedal (eds.)

2009: *Hierarchy. Persistence and Transformation in Social Formations.* New York.

Risley, H. H.

1886: "Primitive marriage in Bengal", in *Asiatic Quarterly Review*, 2: 71-96.

1891 a: "The Study of Ethnology in India", in *Journal of the Anthropological Institute of Great Britain and Ireland*, 20: 235-63.

1891 b: *The Tribes and Castes of Bengal. Ethnographic Glossary*. Calcutta. 2 vols.

1894: "The Progress of Anthropology", in *Imperial and Asiatic Quarterly*, 7: 432-37.

1915 [1908]: *The People of India*. London.

Risley, H. H. and E. A. Gait

1903: *Report on the Census of India 1901*. Calcutta.

Robb, Peter (ed.)

1995: *The Concept of Race in South India*. Delhi.

Roquete, J. I. (ed.)

1842: *Leal Conselheiro, o qual fez Dom Duarte, pela graça de Deos Rei de Portugal e do Algarve.* Paris.

Rose, H. A.

1902: *Census of India, 1901. The Punjab, its Feudatories, and the Nort-West Frontier Province.* Part I. Report. Simla.

Rosenbaum, Alexis

1999: *L'ordre sacré. Les représentations hiérarchiques en philosophie*. Paris.

Ross, Charles

1859: *Correspondence of Charles, First Marquis Cornwallis*. London. 3 vols.

Rosso, Corrado

1980: *Mythe de l'égalité et rayonnement des Lumières*. Pise.

Rousseau, Jean-Jacques

1751: *Discours sur les sciences et les arts*. Genève.

1755: *Discours sur l'origine et les fondements de l'inégalité parmi les hommes*. Amsterdam.

1997: *The Discourses and Other Early Political Writings* (edited and translated by Victor Gourevitch). Cambridge.

Row, T. Ananda

1903: *Census of India 1901. Mysore*. Part I. Report. Bangalore.

Rubiés, Joan-Pau

2000: *Travel and Ethnology in the Renaissance: South India through European Eyes*, 1250-1625. Cambridge.

Russell, R. V.

1902: *Census of India, 1901. Central Provinces*. Part I. Report. Nagpur.

Said, Edward

1978: *Orientalism*. New York,

Schwab, Raymond

1950: *La Renaissance Orientale*. Paris.

Scrafton, Luke

1763: *Reflections on the Government of Indostan; and a Short Sketch of the History of Bengal, from the year 1739 to 1756*. London.

Senart, Emile

1896: *Les castes dans l'Inde: les faits et le système*. Paris.

Shakespear, A.

1848: *Memoir on the Statistics of the North Western Provinces of the Bengal Presidency*. Calcutta.

Sherring, Matthew Atmore

1872: *Hindu Tribes and Castes, as Represented in Benares*. Calcutta.

1879: *Hindu Tribes and Castes, together with an Account of the Mahomedan Tribes of the North-West Frontier and of the Aboriginal Tribes of the Central Provinces*. Calcutta.

1881: *Hindu Tribes and Castes, together with Three Dissertations: on the Natural History of Hindu Caste; the Unity of the Hindu Race; and the Prospects of the Indian Caste*. Calcutta.

Shore, Frederick John

1837: *Notes on Indian Affairs*. London. 2 vols.

Singer, Milton and Bernard S. Cohn (eds.)

1968: *Structure and change in Indian Society*. Chicago.

Sinha, Samita

1993: *Pandits in a Changing Environment. Centres of Sanskrit Learning in Nineteenth Century Bengal*. Calcutta.

Smith, Brian K.

1994: *Classifying the Universe. The Ancient Indian Varṇa System and the Origins of Caste*. New York.

Sonnerat, Pierre

1782: *Voyage aux Indes Orientales et à la Chine*. Paris. 2 vols.

Srinivas, M. N.

1952: *Religion and Society Among the Coorgs of South India*. London.

1955: "The Social System of a Mysore Village", in Marriott, McKim (ed.): 1-35.

1962: *Caste in Modern India and Other Essays*. Bombay.

1966: *Social Change in Modern India*. Berkeley.

1976: *The Remembered Village*. Delhi.

Srinivas, M. N. (ed.)

1955: *India's Villages*. Bombay.

Stevenson, H. N. C.

1954: "Status Evaluation in the Hindu Caste System", in *Journal of the Royal Anthropological Institute,* 84 (1-2): 45-65.

Stirling, A.

1825: "An Account, Geographical, Statistical and Historical of Orissa Proper, or Cuttack", in *Asiatic Researches*, 15: 163-338.

Stokes, Eric

1959: *The English Utilitarians in India*. Oxford.

Stoking, George W. Jr.

1987: *Victorian Anthropology*. New York.

Stuart, H. A.

1893: *Census of India, 1891. Madras.* Report. Madras.

Sweetman, Will

2003: *Mapping Hinduism. "Hinduism" and the Study of Indian Religions 1600-1776*. Halle.

Tarabout, Gilles

1986: *Sacrifier et donner à voir en pays Malabar. Les fêtes de temple au Kerala (Inde du Sud): étude anthropologique.* Paris.

Tavernier, Jean-Baptiste

1675: *Les Six Voyages de Jean Baptiste Tavernier, Écuyer, Baron d'Aubonne, qu'il a fait en Turquie, en Perse et aux Indes.* Paris.

1678: *The Six Voyages of John Baptista Tavernier, a Noble Man of France now Living, through Turky into Peria, and the East-Indies.* London.

Thapar, Romila

2010 (1978): *Ancient Indian Social History. Some Interpretations*. Delhi.

Théré, Christine, Loïc Charles et Jean-Claude Perrot (eds.)

2005: *François Quesnay. Oeuvres économiques complètes et autres textes.* Paris. 2 vols.

Thompson, W. H.

1923: *Census of India, 1921. Bengal.* Part I. Report. Calcutta

Thompson, Edward and G. T. Garratt

1935: *Rise and Fulfilment of British Rule in India*. London.

Thurston, Edgar and K. Rangachari

1909: *Castes and Tribes of Southern India*. Madras. 7 vols.

Toffin, Gérard

1999: "Louis Dumont (1911-1998)", in *L'Homme* 150: 7-13.

Topinard, Paul

1885: *Éléments d'anthropologie générale*. Paris.

1892: "L'Anthropologie du Bengale ou étude des documents anthropométriques recueillis par M. Risley", in *L'Anthropologie*, III: 282-316.

Trautmann, Thomas R.

1997: *Aryans and British India*. Berkeley.

Viroli, Maurizio

1988: *La théorie de la société bien ordonnée chez Jean-Jacques Rousseau*. Berlin.

Vogt, W. Paul

1979: "Un Durkheimien ambivalent: Célestin Bouglé: 1870-1940", in *Revue Française de Sociologie*, 20: 123-139.

Wahnich, Sophie

1997: *L'Impossible citoyen. L'étranger dans la Révolution Française*. Paris.

Ward, William

1815: *A View of the History, Literature and Religion of the Hindoos*. Serampore. 2 vols.

Waterfield, Henry

1875: *Memorandum on the Census of British India 1871-72*. London.

Weber, Max

1958 [1916]: *The Religion of India. The Sciology of Hinduism and Buddhism*. Translated and edited by Hans H. Gerth and Don Martindale. Glencoe.

Weitzman, Sophia

1929: *Warren Hastings and Philip Francis*. Manchester.

Weulersse, G.

1931: *Les Physiocrates*. Paris.

Williams J. Ch.

1869: *The Report of the Census of Oudh.* Vol. I. Lucknow.

Wright, H. R. C.

1954: "Some Aspects of the Permanent Settlement in Bengal", in *The Economic History Review*. New Series, 7 (2): 204-215.

Yalman, Nur

1960: "The Flexibility of Caste Principles in a Kandyan Community", in Leach, E. R. (ed.): 78-112.

1963: "On the Purity of Women in the Castes of Ceylon and Malabar", in *The Journal of the Royal Anthropological Institute of Great Britain and Ireland*, 1: 25-58.

Yang, Anand A.

1987: "A Conversation of Rumors: The Language of Popular 'Mentalités' in Late Nineteenth-Century Colonial India", in *Journal of Social History*, 20 (3): 485-505.

Zumthor, Paul

1954: *Histoire littéraire de la France Médiévale (VIe-XIVe siècles)*. Paris.

INDEX

A

B

C

D

E

F

G

H

I

J

K

L

M

N

O

P

Q

R

S

T

U

V

W

Y

Z